LUCY KIRKWOOD

Lucy Kirkwood's plays include *The Children* (Royal Court); *Chimerica* (Almeida/West End); *NSFW* (Royal Court); *small hours* (co-written with Ed Hime; Hampstead); *Hansel and Gretel*, *Beauty and the Beast* (with Katie Mitchell; National Theatre); *Bloody Wimmin*, as part of *Women, Power and Politics* (Tricycle); *it felt empty when the heart went at first but it is alright now* (Clean Break/Arcola); *Hedda* (Gate, London); *Tinderbox* (Bush). *it felt empty when the heart went at first but it is alright now* won the 2012 John Whiting Award, and was nominated for the Evening Standard Most Promising Playwright Award, and the Susan Smith Blackburn Award. *Chimerica* won the 2014 Olivier Award for Best New Play, the 2013 Evening Standard Best Play Award, the 2014 Critics' Circle Best New Play Award, and the Susan Smith Blackburn Award.

Other Titles in this Series

Lucy Kirkwood

MOSQUITOES

NICK HERN BOOKS

London

www.nickhernbooks.co.uk

A Nick Hern Book

Mosquitoes first published as a paperback original in Great Britain in 2017
by Nick Hern Books Limited, The Glasshouse, 49a Goldhawk Road, London
W12 8QP, in association with the National Theatre, London, by special
arrangement with the Manhattan Theatre Club

Reprinted with revisions in 2017

Mosquitoes copyright © 2017 Lucy Kirkwood

Lucy Kirkwood has asserted her right to be identified as the author of this work

Cover photograph of Olivia Williams and Olivia Colman by David Stewart

Designed and typeset by Nick Hern Books, London
Printed in the UK by CPI Books (UK) Ltd

A CIP catalogue record for this book is available from the British Library

ISBN   978 1 84842 582 8

Mosquitoes was first performed in the Dorfman auditorium of the National Theatre, London, on 25 July 2017 (previews from 18 July). The cast was as follows:

ALICE	Olivia Williams
JENNY	Olivia Colman
THE BOSON	Paul Hilton
LUKE	Joseph Quinn
NATALIE	Sofia Barclay
KAREN	Amanda Boxer
HENRI	Yoli Fuller
JOURNALIST	Vanessa Emme
GAVRIELLA BASTIANELLI/ POLICEWOMAN	Cait Davis
SECURITY GUARD	Ira Mandela Siobhan

Director	Rufus Norris
Designer	Katrina Lindsay
Lighting Designer	Paule Constable
Music	Adam Cork
Sound Designer	Paul Arditti
Video Designers	Finn Ross
	Ian William Galloway
Movement	Ira Mandela Siobhan
Fight Director	Kev McCurdy
Company Voice Work	Charmian Hoare
Staff Director	Nicola Miles-Wildin

Originally commissioned by Manhattan Theatre Club, Lynne Meadow, Artistic Director, Barry Grove, Executive Producer, with funds provided by the Alfred P. Sloan Foundation.

Acknowledgements

This play was a Sloane commission from the Manhattan Theatre Club, and I am very grateful to everyone there who has supported it over the years, especially Annie MacCrae, Lynne Meadow and Doug Hughes.

I would also like to thank:

Rufus Norris.

Mel Kenyon.

The creative team, cast and crew of the National Theatre production.

Connie Potter, Gordon Watts, Paul Laycock and Chris Thomas at CERN who have been so generous and imaginative with their help in the writing of the play.

Lyndsey Turner.

Ben Power.

James Yeatman.

The many actors who have participated in readings.

Yoli Fuller for correcting and improving my appalling French.

Most of all, Ed Hime, for bringing order to chaos.

L.K.

In memory of Alex Willie Singerman

For Sophie

'The general public has long been divided into two parts; those who think that science can do anything and those who are afraid it will.'

Mason & Dixon, Thomas Pynchon

'We are all susceptible to the pull of viral ideas... No matter how smart we get, there is always this deep irrational part that makes us potential hosts for self-replicating information.'

Snow Crash, Neal Stephenson

Characters

THE BOSON
ALICE
JENNY
LUKE
NATALIE
KAREN
HENRI
GAVRIELLA BASTIANELLI/POLICEWOMAN
JOURNALIST
SCIENTISTS

Key

A forward slash (/) indicates an overlap in speech.

Words in brackets are spoken aloud but are incidental.

An asterisk (*) before a line indicates simultaneous speech.

A comma on its own line (,) indicates a beat. A beat is shorter than a pause. It can also denote a shift in thought or energy.

The text has been punctuated to serve the music of the play, not grammatical convention. Dashes are used sparingly and generally indicate a hard interruption.

ACT ONE

IN THE BEGINNING

Summer 2006. A house in Luton, England, beneath a flight path.
JENNY, *heavily pregnant. She walks, always in motion.* ALICE
sits. She is forty-one and JENNY *is thirty-nine.*

JENNY. Just it's like waves.

ALICE. And but which part in particular is worrying you?

JENNY. It's the part which, I think it's mainly the part where it
comes out.

ALICE. This is very natural Jenny.

JENNY. Mike says millions of women do it every day. He says
'look at the animal kingdom'.

JENNY *sits down.*

ALICE. Don't worry about Mike. He's just feeling powerless
and redundant.

JENNY. I want a cigarette.

ALICE. well okay but that's not / going to

JENNY. Mum smoked twenty a day when she was pregnant.

ALICE. Both of us?

JENNY. No just me Alice that's why I'm Forrest Gump and
you're the Wizard of fucking Oz.

ALICE. That's not / what I was

JENNY. Twenty a day. Marlboro, not light. Red. And we're
alright.

*A wave of panic engulfs her. She takes a breath, closes her
eyes, trying to control it.*

ALICE. What?

JENNY. No, it's just. It doesn't kick. I don't feel it, kicking, I think it might be in the wrong position. I think the cord might be round its neck.

ALICE. Okay. Okay. But you've had the ultrasound?

Pause. JENNY *makes a non-committal sound.*

Jenny, you've / had

JENNY. Yeah, it's not, it's not something we felt comfortable doing.

,

ALICE. But. Okay but so because it's completely safe.

JENNY. Um, no, not, actually, not completely

ALICE. In what way?

Pause.

Jenny in / what

JENNY. No because you're going to shout at me.

ALICE. I won't shout at you, when / have I ever

JENNY. They've done animal studies.

,

ALICE. Which animals?

JENNY. Mammals.

Pause.

ALICE. Which mammals?

JENNY. Rats.

ALICE. Rats. Okay. And what did they find in / these

JENNY. Oh you know, just brain injuries. Dyslexia

JENNY *finds a printout of an internet article.*

ALICE. How can a rat be dyslexic?

JENNY. epilepsy (don't do that) mental retardation, an increased incidence in left-handedness in boys

ALICE. Luke is left-handed.

JENNY. well there you go, listen to this:

ALICE. Jenny, we've talked about this.

JENNY. No, I know

ALICE. Googling is

JENNY. Bad, / I know, but just

ALICE. What did we, just because you can access the information doesn't mean you're equipped to understand it.

JENNY. okay, okay but – (*Reading*.) 'a World Health Organisation report warned that ultrasound can cause reduced fetal weight, neurological changes', this is from a journal by the / way, like a proper

ALICE. Millions of women do it, every single day and

JENNY. So? Millions of women drink diet coke.

ALICE. What's wrong with / diet coke?

JENNY. 'In 2001 an ultrasound transducer placed in a woman's uterus recorded sound as loud as a train coming into a station.'

As loud as a *train*.

ALICE. It's safe.

JENNY. As loud as a fucking *train*.

ALICE. In America, you can get it done in a shopping centre.

JENNY. Yeah well in America you can buy a gun in a shopping centre can't you, just cos something happens in America / doesn't mean

ALICE. (oh my God) it's safe, it's safe, it's less dangerous than a hot bath.

JENNY. Yes, well I'd like to believe that Alice / but

ALICE. It doesn't matter whether you believe it, it's a fact.

JENNY. Says who?

ALICE. The doctor, and he's an expert, / so

JENNY. She.

ALICE. She's an expert / so

JENNY. Yeah well I think actually what I feel, *as a mother*, might be stronger than a a a a just a... *fact* don't you?

ALICE. No.

,

JENNY. Okay well there's not like a single version of

ALICE. Yes there is. There is, absolutely / there is

JENNY. Well that's a very Western way / of

ALICE. A what?

JENNY. I'm just / saying.

ALICE. Western?

JENNY. I'm just saying!

ALICE. You live in Luton.

JENNY. Don't, shouting at me, it doesn't kick. It doesn't move. I think it might be dead.

,

ALICE. I promise you. I promise you, there is nothing to worry about.

JENNY. yeah well there's a higher rate of Down's

ALICE. From an ultrasound?

JENNY. No, in IVF babies

ALICE. Statistically?

JENNY. statistically, yes, statistically in IVF babies there is a higher rate of Down's and and and and death.

,

statistically, yes, and all I'm saying is I'm allowed, actually, I am allowed to make my own decisions about what's best for my, without being made to feel like I'm constantly failing some fucking cosmic exam, like I might actually be a capable, grown-up woman you know? Who can be trusted to, not just some sack of skin with a pair of tits for people to to examine

and and inject and monitor and and stick their fucking fingers
in because actually at the end of the day who's in charge?
Who's in charge?

,

fucking, statistically, who's in charge, / Alice?

ALICE. You are.

JENNY. Thank you. Not them. Not you. Me. That's all I'm.
Thank you.

JENNY *looks at* ALICE, *wretched*.

Didn't you ever feel like this?

ALICE. I'm sorry, I wish I could... but actually I felt. Sort of
amazing. Like, tuned in to some weird frequency, because
I understood for the first time. This is what my body is for,
and it was like. Wow! / And

JENNY. Yeah and your boobs got really big, and then one day
you sneezed and out popped Luke, and he trotted off the bed
and cut his own umbilical cord. I bet you didn't even shit
yourself / did you?

ALICE. Stop it. You know that's not

JENNY. That's not?

ALICE. no, you know that's not

JENNY. Tell me then.

ALICE. I already told you.

JENNY. So tell me again.

Pause.

The contractions started, go on. Please. Please Alice.

Pause.

Please

ALICE. The contractions started at about 10 p.m.

JENNY. But which this worried you because it was too early.

ALICE. Yes it was much too early. I hadn't even packed my
case so I instead I put some things

JENNY. Knickers, nightie, inhaler.

ALICE. I shoved them in a plastic bag and I called the ambulance.

JENNY. You get to the hospital, then – no I forgot, this is the best bit, go on.

ALICE. The midwife / was a

JENNY. The midwife was a man!

ALICE. I nearly said No. I don't want you, I want a woman because this is a very exposing process and also

JENNY. and also he was really fit, you said.

ALICE. yes and also he was problematically good looking, but then he said is your husband or partner on his or her way?

JENNY. And you said no actually he's in Geneva watching protons collide cos that apparently is more important than the birth / of his

ALICE. No I just said no and he understood because Javier was a very understanding person and married with a girl of his own that he delivered in a beautiful ceremony in a Donald Duck paddling pool.

JENNY. And you're still just on the gas and air at this point.

ALICE. No Pethidine too, I was six centimetres.

JENNY. The Grand Canyon!

ALICE. But then his heartbeat slowed down. And they said we'll have to do a Caesarean. I didn't wake up till later. I thought, Luke wasn't there so / I thought

JENNY. Course you did, baby's not there, of course you thought

ALICE. Nurse comes in, she says: You can see him now

JENNY. no but before that she says.

,

ALICE. yes she said do you have a Faith? She said Do you have a Faith? Because if you have a Faith and / it I just

JENNY. no then you said What kind?

ALICE. literally didn't understand the question

JENNY. and then you did

ALICE. and then I did I understood it completely I started crying ran out, well not ran, I couldn't run

JENNY. waddled.

ALICE. and then I found him.

Pause.

JENNY. Go on.

,

ALICE. He was in a closed-air bassinette. That's what they called it / but

JENNY. But it was an incubator

ALICE. Yes. A plastic box, you could see through the sides.

JENNY. You couldn't touch him.

You couldn't touch him, could you?

This is making me feel a lot better, you couldn't touch / him

ALICE. I couldn't touch him, I had to put my hands into these gloves to touch him.

JENNY. His head.

ALICE. His head was the size of an apple.

,

JENNY *feels her stomach.*

JENNY. It kicked.

,

Feel then.

Pause. ALICE *puts her hand on* JENNY.

Wait. Might do it again in a minute.

They sit, waiting.

THE CREATION

THE BOSON *appears.*
He should be visible in every scene-change. But he is visible
only to us.
He is holding an apple. The apple explodes.
A Big Bang. Very loud and frightening.
A pea-souper of plasma settles over the stage.

THE BOSON. There are two types of physicist. Theoretical

He gestures to himself.

and Experimental

He gestures to ALICE.

in the beginning there was
you and me and nothing else only
an enormous amount of energy
(yours mainly)
and even though we had talked the theory round the houses
the child existed on paper for years
in the end the experiment was uncontrolled, and the
scientists were drunk, in darkness in love in exhaustion in
a rented room as
chaos
began to order itself inside you into

THE BOSON *makes* LUKE, *sixteen, appear, at home in*
Geneva, at his laptop, wearing headphones. THE BOSON
watches him.

Your friend request has been accepted.

THE BOSON *exits.*

VIRAL

Lights up on NATALIE, *sixteen.*

LUKE. hi Natalie, thanks for accepting me

NATALIE. hey Luke thanks for finding me! It was so cool of you to sit with me at lunch yesterday I felt like such a loner!!! But I couldn't find you today, WTF?

LUKE. sorry. I'm on suspension

NATALIE. shit what did you do?

LUKE. hacked the parent portal

NATALIE. that's hilarious. You're lucky, you could've got expelled

LUKE. I was trying to get expelled

NATALIE. oh right. That backfired then didn't it? LOL

LUKE. LOL

NATALIE. what you doing?

LUKE. thinking about killing myself so I don't have to do my French homework

NATALIE. ha ha what is it?

LUKE. past participle

NATALIE. omg the past participle is like, the *devil*. But you just have to remember which verbs are être and which ones are avoir

LUKE. do you miss your old school?

NATALIE. also don't forget it has to agree with the subject when the auxiliary is être sorry crossed over yeah I do, we move all the time for my dad's job and he says it's good to learn to adapt yourself to new situations but he doesn't get how exhausting it is making friends all the time? You know those guys from the drama club? Stefan and Heloise and Celeste? I tried to ask them about auditions today and they literally like laughed in my face

LUKE. yeah those guys are dicks

NATALIE. yeah and also is 'neger' not as racist as it sounds cos
I heard them say it about Mahalia

LUKE. no it's totally racist. What does your dad do?

NATALIE. he works for UBS. He's an investment manager, he
like, manages investments. How come you're in Geneva?

LUKE. my mum's a scientist, she's looking for the Higgs boson

NATALIE. what's that?

LUKE. it's just a particle. It's invisible but it's all around us.
They think it's what gives us mass. Alice bangs on about it
all the time, she's completely obsessed. I think she might get
married again. This wankstain keeps coming round and
leaving the bread out of the fridge and sometimes they have
showers together which I think is completely unnecessary

NATALIE. my parents are divorced too it sucks. Do you still
see your dad?

Pause.

LUKE. not really. He works for a government science agency.

NATALIE. cool. Like in *Men in Black 2*?

or *Men in Black 1*

or

LUKE. i'm not really allowed to talk about it. It's classified.

NATALIE. cool. Did you know there's a video of you going
mental in the canteen on youtube?

LUKE. I wasn't going mental. Stefan put spätzle in my backpack

NATALIE. I spend like five hours a night on youtube that's
really bad isn't it? Does Stefan have a girlfriend?

LUKE. I don't know

NATALIE. him and Heloise are just friends right? Have you
seen the video with the man crying and going 'Leave her
alone! Leave Britney alone!'?

LUKE. no

NATALIE. omg you need to youtube it immediately, have you seen the one about how you can charge your iPod with an onion?

LUKE. yeah but it's not true

NATALIE. I know I totally spazzed my Nano have you seen the one where all the prisoners do the dance from 'Thriller'?

LUKE. no

NATALIE. have you seen two girls one cup?

LUKE. no

NATALIE. don't it's rank

LUKE. have you seen the one where the baby's just laughing and laughing?

NATALIE. NO. Oh my god BRB

The sound of a baby laughing and laughing and laughing. Pause.

LUKE. hey did you watch it?

Pause.

so cute right?

Pause.

poke

NATALIE. HEY LUKE I WANT 2 SUCK YOUR FREAKY COCK YUM YUM

Pause.

oh my god sorry I'm at Celeste's I left my laptop for like one second to go to the toilet, we made vodka jelly she's so wasted!!!!!

LUKE. oh. Cool. Ha ha

hey have you seen the one where the three year old explains *Stars Wars*? Here's / the

NATALIE. Heloise says your mum's gonna make a black hole

A faint hum of mosquitoes.

LUKE. what?

NATALIE. seriously it's on the news

LUKE. where?

NATALIE. BBC website. And the *New York Times*. It says the machine they're building will make black holes that eat the earth

LUKE. yeah well at least she's not evicting poor people from their houses. Joke.

NATALIE. yeah I know my mum says my dad is the banal face of evil but he still pays for all her shit so.

LUKE. ha. does his office use microsoft windows?

NATALIE. why

LUKE. be easy then

NATALIE. what would?

LUKE. put a virus in their operating system. Shut them down for a week

NATALIE. shut up

,

seriously?

LUKE. yeah. If you want

NATALIE. Heloise says you're chatting shit

LUKE. why are you even talking to Heloise about it she doesn't know what the fuck she's talking about she had to take year 8 twice and she thinks techno is good music why would i say i could do it if i couldn't do it i can do it in like three days

…

Natalie did you get my last message?

…

…

hey Natalie, you there?

The humming grows.

…

…

hey Natalie. Are u ok?

…

I'm not being nasty but it's actually really rude just to completely not reply to messages from someone when they delete delete delete delete delete delete delete

…

dear Natalie. I hope you are well. I've been really busy so sorry if I've missed any messages from you. Just wondered if you could check something for me? I'm on irregular verbs in the future tense, how do you say, 'I will be back at 4 p.m.?'

Pause.

NATALIE. Je serai de retour à seize heures

LUKE. hey! How are you, thanks so much, that's what I thought, what about 'Next summer, she will go to the French Riviera'?

NATALIE. L'été prochain, elle ira sur la Côte d'Azur

LUKE. 'We will have three children'

NATALIE. Nous aurons trois enfants

LUKE. 'You will be safe and sound'

NATALIE. Vous serez sains et saufs

The humming grows oppressively loud.

LUKE. thanks you're a lifesaver. I'm back at school on Monday. I was thinking we / could

NATALIE. sorry can't chat now. Stefan and Heloise and Celeste and me are going to see *Ratatouille*

Pause.

LUKE. cool. seen it already. it's shit, by the way I finished that thing.

I could do it today only I need to get into your dad's email and you probably don't know his password

Pause.

Natalie?

The mosquitoes hum. Loud and oppressive. ALICE *enters, coat, suitcase.*

VACUUM

ALICE *talks but we can't hear what she's saying, until...*

LUKE *takes his headphones off. The humming cuts.*

ALICE. love.

LUKE. What?

ALICE. Auntie Jenny sends her love.

LUKE. Has she got bowel cancer?

ALICE. What? No.

LUKE. No just you said it was an emergency so

ALICE. An emotional emergency not a medical. She's fine. Amy's fine. She's nearly crawling now. Jenny was just a bit frightened darling.

LUKE. 'Kay well I'm frightened too. I'm frightened about people who fly from Switzerland to Luton just cos their sister's a retard. / You left the light on in your room again so.

ALICE. We don't use that word, I was rushing to catch the plane.

LUKE. Fine, you'll be dead by the time the coal runs out so you probably don't give a shit.

ALICE. I do give a. I do.

LUKE. It's going to use more electricity than the whole of Geneva, you know that?

ALICE. What is?

LUKE. Your machine. Your experiment, and it's going to make a black hole

ALICE *laughs*.

ALICE. The possibility of us making a black hole is one tenth of a millionth billionth billionth of one per cent.

,

LUKE. Right. So you're saying there is a chance?

ALICE. What's happened? What's the matter?

LUKE. Why do you always pretend like you don't know? I've told you, like repeatedly, I hate that fucking school.

ALICE. Don't swear at me. Please do not swear at me, / I don't like it.

LUKE. Jenny swears at you, Jenny swears / at you like, constantly and

ALICE. Well Auntie Jenny is not someone you need to be imitating.

LUKE. You think she's stupid.

ALICE. No, I / never

LUKE. You said she was epically thick.

ALICE. *No*, what / I said was

LUKE. You said it was incredible she managed to put her shoes on in the morning.

ALICE. That's enough.

LUKE. Please tell me we don't have to go there for Christmas this year.

ALICE. Not this year, no.

LUKE *thanks the heavens*.

I mean they'll probably come here.

LUKE. You're not serious.

ALICE. Don't you want to meet your cousin?

LUKE. Yeah but you can't put a baby on a plane.

ALICE. You can. Of course you can, that age, a baby's very portable, I got you a Toblerone from duty-free.

She takes the Toblerone from her bag and gives it to him.

LUKE. Sorry, what did you want?

ALICE. Just to. Say hello.

LUKE. Hello.

ALICE. Hello.

LUKE. Hello.

ALICE. Hello.

> ,

Why don't I / just

LUKE. Goodbye.

LUKE puts his headphones on.

ALICE. have a bit of a tidy in here

LUKE. I don't want you touching my stuff, goodbye.

ALICE. it's a bit, / the plates and the food it's a bit unhygienic and it smells a little it smells a bit

LUKE. it's my stuff I don't want you going through my stuff, I've asked you politely / Alice.

ALICE. it smells a bit like death sweetheart!

She laughs.

Sorry but. There is a smell – Luke can you take the headphones off.

> ,

Take the headphones off please Luke.

> ,

Take the headphones off please.

She reaches for them, he bats her away. Pause.

I know you can hear me. I wanted to show you something.

ALICE *takes her laptop out of her bag and starts it up.*

So we can't start testing for the Higgs until the LHC starts up. But what we know already, is what it will look like if it is there.

She looks for a response, doesn't get one, ploughs on.

Okay so we use the ATLAS software to convert the data into 'objects' and you can use those objects to reconstruct particles which I know it sounds very complicated but then you use those particles to make an algorithm, / which

LUKE. I see.

ALICE. and then you can make a sound a track of sound! Sorry?

LUKE *takes the headphones off.*

LUKE. I said I see.

ALICE. I knew you'd. This is how NASA listens to the Sun. The programme we bought. For your birthday. There's a competition, I thought you might

LUKE. I have exams.

ALICE. yes but for fun. You don't play me your music any more.

LUKE. You don't shave your armpits. Embarrassing. Just don't come to school if you're / going to whatever just forget it.

ALICE. Luke.

,

The competition is you take the samples and remix, that's the, isn't it, you remix the sounds into a track, a musical track. I think you'd be absolutely brilliant at it, and there's a prize.

LUKE. What's the prize?

ALICE. I'm not sure. But there definitely is one.

ALICE *clicks on her laptop. A sample plays. A strange, beautiful, metallic sound.*

That's the sound of a Higgs jet decaying.

They listen.

LUKE. If you find it, d'you think he'll come back?

A long pause.

ALICE. No. No I don't.

LUKE. But he worked on it. He worked on it for / like

ALICE. I know but – it's a bit difficult to.

Pause.

LUKE. What?

ALICE. No, it's. He thought, he had begun to think that when we discovered the Higgs potential, it would demonstrate that the universe is inherently unstable and destined to fall apart.

,

LUKE. Do you think that?

ALICE. It's not something I worry about, no. It wouldn't happen for billions of years. And what we're talking about, a vacuum bubble, expanding at the speed of light, you'd never even know about it.

LUKE. Why?

ALICE. Well. Because you'd be dead.

,

LUKE. Oh well that's alright then.

She laughs. He laughs.

ALICE. He was just like that. He could be quite bleak and, I mean, he thought a *lot* about how the universe could end! You're not like that at all.

LUKE. What does that mean?

ALICE. What?

LUKE. Why would you say that, 'you're not like that'?

ALICE. Because you're not.

Pause. LUKE *goes back to his laptop. Puts his headphones on.*

You're so clever. I wish you wanted to create things, not destroy them.

THE BOSON *enters and watches them.*

The sound of vast building works.

Over this, a baby's cry, growing in volume.

ACT TWO

REPEATEDLY, AND AT REGULAR INTERVALS

One year later. Geneva, September 2008. JENNY, now forty-one, in her coat. Her case at her feet. Her stomach flat. ALICE, now forty-three, sits. Emo music is playing at volume offstage.

JENNY. I'm on the aisle. I said to Mum, go on the aisle because of her legs but she wanted the window so I'm on the aisle, that's how I can see him. Long black shirt. Baggy black trousers. Little… hat. And what gets my attention is he's not *doing anything*. Hasn't got a book, not watching TV, he's just staring. Straight ahead.

ALICE. Frightened to fly probably. Luke! Can you turn it down please?

The music goes off. Over the following, JENNY unzips her case, takes out a duty-free carton of cigarettes, takes one pack out, takes a cigarette out of that and lights it.

JENNY. This is what I'm thinking only then: *he checks his watch*. He checks his watch repeatedly and *at regular intervals*. Then he goes up the back to the loo. And what I notice is he *takes his passport with him*.

LUKE, *now seventeen, enters with mugs of tea, gives them to* JENNY *and* ALICE.

ALICE. Thanks darling.

LUKE. You can't smoke in the apartment.

ALICE. It's alright, / just this once.

JENNY. And a minute later (thanks Al) he comes / back so I

LUKE. So we just breathe that in do we?

ALICE. Luke, please / don't.

JENNY. So I get up to use the toilet and –

> LUKE *coughs, pointed.* JENNY *throws her cigarette in her mug.*

> So I get up to use the toilet, well. The toilet now has an *out-of-order sign on it* which okay fine but: this chap's been up there a minute before me, right? So my question is: who put that sign up? And why, so this is when I say to Mum, Mum look at this guy, he's a bit odd. And she agrees he is *a bit odd. And this is when the second man gets up and goes to the back.* I'm a bag of snakes, so I find the stewardess and I (quietly) I say to her there is a man, a *pair of men*, and I tell her about the checking the watch, and the not watching television, and half of me's thinking, she's going to laugh, and half of me's thinking 'we're all going to die'. But you know what Alice?

> ,

> You know what Alice?

ALICE. What?

JENNY. She *thanked me*. She said 'thank you madam, we depend on the vigilance of our customers'.

LUKE. Were they Asian?

JENNY. That isn't the point the / point is

LUKE. But were they?

ALICE. Luke, pack it in.

JENNY. I'd rather be a racist than die in a plane crash.

ALICE. Jen, it's okay. What you've been through is enough to –

JENNY. And what I'm thinking now is okay it's me it's worst-case scenario Jenny and ha ha let's all laugh and call her a bigot.

> But I watched that stewardess as we landed.

> She was white as a sheet.

> ,

> (*To* LUKE.) I bought you a Toblerone.

JENNY *takes a big Toblerone from her bag. Gives it to* LUKE.

ALICE. A Toblerone! Jen that's so, say thank you to Auntie Jenny.

LUKE. Thank you to Auntie Jenny.

JENNY. Give your mad old aunt a kiss then.

LUKE *looks at* ALICE. *She gives him daggers.* LUKE *goes to* JENNY. *Pecks her cheek.* JENNY *grabs him and holds him tightly.* LUKE *wriggles, she lets go.*

(*To* ALICE.) Got you something too. Didn't forget you.

She goes back to her suitcase, takes two bottles of red wine out.

ALICE. You didn't have / to

She takes four more bottles out. She takes a bottle of vodka out.

JENNY. Yeah well so cheap duty-free, false economy not to really.

She takes out a bottle of Crème de Menthe.

ALICE. What's that?

JENNY. Crème de Menthe. Was on offer. Got a free glass with it. Could have a little one now if you like. See the day in.

ALICE. It's 8 a.m.

JENNY. I know it's 8 a.m. I was joking wasn't I. Do you think you actually have to tell me that, 'it's 8 a.m.', is that something you think you actually have to, Jesus Alice, because it turns out I am not actually you know, Oliver fucking Reed so.

KAREN (*off*). Alice. Do you have such a thing as a padded hanger?

ALICE *exits.* JENNY *looks at* LUKE. *Sniffs.*

JENNY. Don't take this the wrong way but your mum's a patronising bitch sometimes.

She takes a swig. Offers it to LUKE. *He shakes his head.*

What's this boyfriend like then?

LUKE. I don't know.

JENNY. You don't know! What, big handsome French man comes round every day and you look the other way! No, it's difficult though isn't it? But you want your mum to be happy, don't you? I was hoping you'd come over with her for the, for the, you know for the funeral.

LUKE. I don't fly.

JENNY. No I know, very sensible! I just thought. You might regret it. Not saying goodbye. Properly, I'm not having a go.
,

D'you remember when we came for Christmas? D'you remember playing with her on the blue rug?

LUKE. Yeah.

JENNY. You remember it do you? You remember her?

LUKE. Yeah.

JENNY. Yeah you were such a help, I can't tell you, honestly, you were brilliant, doing that thing, with the sock. Making her laugh. You'll be a lovely daddy.

LUKE. I'm not having kids.

JENNY. Well not yet I hope!

LUKE. The earth's already overpopulated. By the time I'm sixty there'll be nine billion people. Most of them will starve to death.

JENNY. Ooh, cheerful! You sound like your dad.

LUKE. Do I?

JENNY. Yeah. Yeah, anyway, you don't mind giving Granny Karen your bed for a few days do you?

LUKE. A bit.

JENNY. Ooh, an honest man, I like that!

LUKE. Where's Uncle Mike?

JENNY. Uncle Mike's taking some time, sweetheart.

LUKE. Has he left you?

JENNY. No! Listen to this one, 'has he – ', no, he's just taking some time. Bit of R and R!

LUKE. Away from you?

JENNY. We're taking some time apart, thank you nosy parker.

LUKE. But whose decision was it?

JENNY. Joint, it was a joint decision. Shall we have a bit of that Toblerone, I had my breakfast at 5 a.m.

LUKE. Is it because of Amy?

JENNY. Just fuck off Luke.

ALICE *enters, helping* KAREN, *who walks on a frame.*

KAREN. Did she tell you? I told her to leave those poor men alone but would she listen? Scared that poor stewardess half to death.

LUKE *makes to exit.*

ALICE. Where are you going?

LUKE. Um, school?

KAREN. I saw them at passport control. They were taken to a small room.

ALICE. Well say goodbye.

KAREN. A *small room.*

LUKE. 'Kay, bye.

ALICE. Wish me luck.

LUKE. Good luck.

LUKE *exits.* JENNY *lights a cigarette.*

KAREN. And it'll go on their records you know. Every time they fly from now on it'll be cavity searches and small rooms. I don't know how I raised such a fearful creature.

ALICE. Okay Mum. That's enough.

HENRI enters. JENNY clocks him. KAREN doesn't.

KAREN. Handsome they were. Omar Sharif handsome.

JENNY. Shut up Mum.

JENNY stares at HENRI.

Bon jour.

ALICE. Um, this is Henri.

HENRI. Hello. Welcome to Geneva. (*To* KAREN.) You must be Alice's sister, I think.

As he kisses her on each cheek, KAREN *screams with laughter, hits him playfully.*

KAREN. Oh, don't!

He turns to JENNY.

HENRI. And this is the famous Granny Karen, yes?

JENNY stares back.

JENNY. Is this sposed to be charming? That what you're going for, charm? 'Hello. Nice to meet you.' That's what people usually start with.

He is suddenly serious, holds her hands.

HENRI. Jenny forgive me. I am so sorry for your suffering. You have been in our prayers.

He embraces her. Warm. Kind. JENNY *doesn't know what to do with it.*

(*To* ALICE.) Your son put my toothbrush in the toilet again.

ALICE. Oh no. That's not. There's a spare under the sink.

HENRI. If you still want a lift, we leave in eight-and-a-half minutes.

ALICE laughs. HENRI *exits.*

KAREN. He'll do.

JENNY. Eight-and-a-half minutes. Does he time everything to the second?

ALICE. It was a private – he's joking, he's being funny.

JENNY. Oh right. Cos that went over my head. Must be a whole new level of comedy I just don't get, I thought you said he was handsome.

ALICE. I'm sorry. I have to go to work. I have to be there by nine, if it was any / other

KAREN. It's the big day, I know! The grand switching-on!

JENNY. Shit, that's today? You should have said.

ALICE. You've had / other things to

JENNY. Why didn't you say?

KAREN. The first beam! I'd like to come with you.

ALICE. Why don't you stay here, keep Jenny company? You could see the Jardin Anglais, Luke loves the Jardin Anglais, there's a clock made of flowers and / you can

KAREN. A clock made of flowers, Jenny! You'll like that. (*To* ALICE.) I'll put on some slacks and powder my nose, be ready for you in a flash.

ALICE. Just it might be tricky at this late / stage to

KAREN. I should have won a Nobel Prize. I think they can find me a corner of the room.

KAREN *exits.* ALICE *goes to* JENNY. JENNY *bats her away.*

JENNY. Don't.

ALICE. What?

JENNY. I didn't know it was today.

ALICE. It's all over the news.

JENNY. Oh is it? I'm so sorry I'm not up to date with current / affairs

ALICE. Sorry, sorry, what did I do wrong here? You ring me up, in tears, you need to get away I say / of course, come

JENNY. You should have said, it's not convenient.

ALICE. You're in grief! You're / my sister and you're in grief

JENNY. We would have come another day.

ALICE. You'd already booked the tickets!

JENNY. No just, crazy but I thought you might take some time off.

ALICE. I've been working on this for *eleven / years*

JENNY. Eleven years, I know, eleven years, know what I was working on for eleven years? Having a fucking kid, but whatever, you have to go, so go, I'm just saying if you'd said it wasn't a good time

ALICE. It is a good time.

JENNY. Well not if you're never going to be here it's not, might / as well be sitting at home in fucking Luton

ALICE. I am going to be here, just not every single minute of every / single day!

JENNY. Did I ask for that? Did I ask for every single minute? No.

ALICE *sighs, heavy.* JENNY *mimics the sigh. Tuts, viciously irritated.*

A long pause. KAREN *enters, still in a skirt/dress. Takes in the silence.*

KAREN. Oh dear. The permafrost descends. Already, how long have we...

She looks at her watch.

Forty minutes! Some sort of a record, right girls?

JENNY. Yeah you'd think with your soothing maternal presence we'd make it to lunch at least. Fuckssake can you hear yourself?

KAREN *shakes her head, looks at* ALICE, *gestures to* JENNY.

KAREN. You see this? You hear this? And she can't understand
why I need some time out.

ALICE. Mum. Come on. Jenny's feeling / very

JENNY. JENNY'S NOT FEELING ANYTHING.

Pause. ALICE *looks at* KAREN.

ALICE. I thought you wanted to change?

KAREN *looks down at herself. A confusion. Pause*.

KAREN. I changed. I changed my mind. Hey Alice. Got one
for you.

Allie.

Pause.

Oi.

ALICE. Yes Mum.

KAREN. Okay so Heisenberg is driving in his car when
a policeman pulls him over for speeding. The policeman
asks: 'Do you know how fast you were going?' Heisenberg
replies: 'No. But I know where I am!'

KAREN *cracks up*. ALICE *smiles*.

JENNY. Why is that funny?

HENRI *enters, dressed, with the car keys*.

HENRI. On y va?

ALICE. You want to wait in the car with Henri, / Mum?

HENRI. Avec plaisir. Après-vous madame.

KAREN *takes* HENRI*'s arm and they go*.

JENNY. Excuse me? Why is that funny?

ALICE. You wouldn't get it.

JENNY. Not an imbecile, not a fucking halfwit

ALICE. Never said you / were it's just

JENNY. So go on then.

ALICE. complicated to explain.

JENNY. Have a go.

ALICE. I can't. I'm late. I'm sorry.

Pause.

Don't mind Luke. He doesn't understand. He cried when
I told him.

You will. You will be gentle with him, won't you?

Sudden black.

LA FIN DU MONDE EST REPORTÉE

*The ATLAS control room. Screens, a crowd, a great clamour,
cameras, laptops. A* TV JOURNALIST *is mic'd up, preparing
to broadcast to a* CAMERAMAN. *She should be the nationality
of the country in which the play is being performed.*
SCIENTISTS *enter speaking in many different languages.*

GAVRIELLA. Ho bisogno di caffè ma non l'ha portato
nessuna… e neppure qualcosa da mangiare… come stanno
funzionando le macchine? Sei pronto! Susuma?

JOURNALIST. Can someone talk to me?

FRENCH SCIENTIST. Oui oui, je suis dans la salle de contrôle
je dois verifier quelque chose avant qu'on commence…

JOURNALIST. Can someone please talk to me?

CAMERAMAN. Hallo? Hörst du mich? Ja ich komme.

Pause.

JOURNALIST. Yeah I can hear you fine. Okay. Stand by.

ALICE and KAREN *enter,* KAREN *walks slowly with
a stick.*

KAREN. You don't expect the decay.

ALICE. You're not decaying.

KAREN. I wasn't referring to myself. I was referring to the rust.

ALICE. It's not rust, it's wood.

ALICE *brings* KAREN *a chair, she slumps gratefully into it. A* SCIENTIST *approaches* ALICE.

FRENCH SCIENTIST. Alice, viens voir! Ils nous ont mis dans le Google doodle!

ALICE. Oh my God! Montre-moi...

They rush away to look, as GAVRIELLA BASTIANELLI *approaches* KAREN.

KAREN. I'm out of the game.

GAVRIELLA. Fatti non foste a viver come bruti – a viver...

KAREN. I forget everything takes an eternity to get going. The waiting. Alice.

JOURNALIST. Armageddon. Armageddon.

CAMERAMAN. Ich bin bereit ich erwartete auf die zweite batterie

JOURNALIST. Am I saying that right? 'Armageddon'?

FRENCH SCIENTIST. Gavriella, il y a beaucoup trop de monde ici. Tu peux faire quelque chose s'il te plaît?

GAVRIELLA. Fare il tuo sporco lavoro non è compito mio. (*To* KAREN.) Madam, do you mind if I move you to the side?

KAREN *looks at her. Pause.*

KAREN. I have a first-class honours degree from the Imperial College of Science and a DPhil from the University of Oxford, in 1956 I received a research fellowship to Cambridge, where I was instrumental to pioneering theories into condensed matter, particularly the liquid helium which I believe has such import to the function of this Collider, and which won my husband the Nobel Prize, in 1975 I received a Leverhulme Trust grant and vastly expanded existing knowledge of carbon nanotubes, I have been Treasurer of the Royal Society, I am the recipient of the Glazebrook Medal, the Faraday Prize and thirteen, one-three, honorary degrees, I am a foreign member of the American Academy of Arts and Sciences and since my retirement I have written two widely acclaimed books.

In short, yes. I do mind being moved to the side.

ALICE *rushes over.*

ALICE. Mum, this is Gavriella Bastianelli, my partner, she's in my working group, Gavriella, my mother.

They shake hands.

GAVRIELLA. The famous Karen Landau, yes, I came to your lectures at Cornell in 2001. Alice has told you about our work improving the triggers?

KAREN. We don't talk shop. Her sister sulks. All these computers! When I started out it was me and three men in eggy pullovers, sitting in the back of a van in a field somewhere in Cambridgeshire. You really felt you were on an adventure.

JOURNALIST (*to* CAMERAMAN). because we'd both had a lot to drink and

ALICE *sweeps past, the* JOURNALIST *thrusts a mic in her face.*

'scuse me? Do you have any comment to make about the potentially dangerous work due to take place here in Geneva now the LHC is online?

ALICE. well I don't know if I'd phrase it quite like / that but

JOURNALIST. Okay but if I can just, in September 2007 they said the risk of a destructive incident was zero.

ALICE. Yes?

JOURNALIST. But in October that same year they said the risk was negligible.

ALICE. That's correct.

JOURNALIST. Can you look towards the camera?

ALICE *looks towards the camera.*

ALICE. That's correct.

JOURNALIST. Negligible isn't zero.

ALICE. Scientifically speaking, it's as good as.

JOURNALIST. Do you admit that the LHC is not one-hundred-per-cent safe?

ALICE. You can't know that anything is definitely safe.

JOURNALIST. So there is a risk.

ALICE. Studies show that particles collide at higher speeds in the natural world than we could ever hope to emulate at our facility. Studies have proved the end is not nigh. Excuse me.

ALICE *moves off, rejoins* KAREN *and* GAVRIELLA.

KAREN. Is this it? Is something happening?

GAVRIELLA. They're about to send the first beam, watch.

They look up at the screens, waiting,

JOURNALIST. This is Lara Gallagher live from the Large Hadron Collider in Geneva, Switzerland, as it goes online for the first time. The largest experiment in human history and one that, some say, *could* bring Armageddon. In just a moment, beams of protons will be fired around the pipe beneath our feet, in mankind's most ambitious attempt to understand how the universe began. But it also brings fears it could become a 'black hole factory', threatening life on earth. We're just waiting for the first beam now.

LYN EVAN*'s Welsh lilt is heard. Perhaps he is voiced by* THE BOSON.

EVANS. Let's get started everybody. Now comes the day of reckoning.

A tense hush falls over the room.

Five, four, three, two, one. Now.

Pause. Nothing.

No beam.

ALICE *puts her hand over mouth. She is shocked and grief-stricken, like the* SCIENTISTS *around her.*

KAREN. Oh, what a let-down.

JOURNALIST (*to* CAMERAMAN). Okay, back to me.

ALICE. What happened?

GAVRIELLA *shakes her head, distraught.*

GAVRIELLA. I don't know.

JOURNALIST. Back to me. Back to me.

EVANS. Okay. Let's try again.

ALICE *reaches for* GAVRIELLA*'s hand, they clasp each other.*

Five. Four. Three. Two. One. Zero.

A very long pause. Finally a tiny beep. A bright pulse of light.

Yes! Yes!

An explosion of joy in the control room. Celebration. Applause. Camera flashes.

ALICE. Yes!

JOURNALIST. The first beam! That's it, that's the first beam we just saw there.

GAVRIELLA *makes a call on her mobile.*

KAREN. Was that it?

ALICE. I think so, do we have confirmation?

GAVRIELLA (*on phone*). Hey, are you seeing anything?

GAVRIELLA *listens and puts her hand over the phone, excited.*

Susuma found a signal in the liquid argon calorimeter.

ALICE. Are you sure?

GAVRIELLA. Yes, the timing matches the trigger perfectly.

They embrace.

JOURNALIST. Excuse me? Can you explain to us what just happened?

GAVRIELLA. The beam is on its way!

ALICE. Can I borrow your phone? I left mine at home.

GAVRIELLA *gives it to her.*

JOURNALIST. And what does that actually mean?

GAVRIELLA. It means we are in business.

ALICE (*into phone*). We have beam Luke! There are bottles of champagne all over the desks. I wish I could show you.

KAREN. I always think it must sound like violence.

ALICE. What?

KAREN. The language we use. Impact, collisions. It sounds like runaway trains doesn't it. Car crashes. When all we're talking about is, what? The force of two mosquitoes, flying into each other.

She flies her index fingers together, makes a gentle noise as they impact.

I need the lavatory.

JOURNALIST. This is Lara Gallagher returning you to the studio, do keep your texts coming in on today's topic, 'Are scientists playing God with our planet's safety?' Next up we hear from the Manchester mum who claims a standard X-ray procedure left her son speaking with a Russian accent. That, and more, after the break.

Sudden black.

AN EQUAL AND OPPOSITE FORCE

ALICE's *apartment. The space fugged with cigarette smoke.
A full ashtray on the floor. A glass of green liquid beside it.*
LUKE *enters. In a state, he's been beaten up, his nose is
bleeding. He's shaking. He picks up the glass. Examines it.
Takes a sip.*

JENNY *enters. Watches him. He takes out his phone, dials.*

JENNY. Thought you were a burglar.

He hangs up abruptly. She fiddles with an iPhone.

D'you know the passcode for your mum's phone?

LUKE. Yeah.

,

JENNY. What is it then?

LUKE. Why've you got her phone?

He turns. JENNY *sees his injuries for the first time.*

JENNY. Jesus, what happened to you?

LUKE. It's nothing. Is that my hoodie?

JENNY. It's not nothing, who did that to you?

LUKE. Did you go in my room?

JENNY. Of course I went in your room. They left me here, on
my own, what'm I sposed to do, stare at / the walls?

LUKE. Why did you go in my room?

JENNY. I wanted to read your diary, who did this?

LUKE. I don't have a diary, take / it off.

JENNY. Well I know that now. Come here.

LUKE. No, take it off.

She sighs, takes it off. Tosses it to him. He smells it.

Great. Now it stinks.

JENNY. Sit down.

LUKE *doesn't sit. Pause.*

What was it, a fight?

A long pause. No answer. JENNY *goes out.*

LUKE *takes out his phone, dials.*

LUKE. Hi, it's me... um, Luke. I just wanted to say, uh, sorry. I'm really sorry Natalie, I didn't mean to

LUKE *hangs up as* JENNY *returns with a wet cloth. She starts to dab at his cuts. He flinches away. She gives him a look. He lets her clean him up. Their faces are close. He watches her. Pause.*

JENNY. I punched someone once.

LUKE. At school?

JENNY. No, it was in a Wetherspoons, I was about... thirty-two? We'd been trying for about four years. She told me if I couldn't have kids then my life would be rich in other ways, who's Natalie?

LUKE. Don't listen to my calls.

JENNY. Girlfriend?

LUKE. She's no one. She's the only English girl in my year. She helps me with French sometimes, okay? Is the interrogation over?

JENNY. This isn't an interrogation. This is just... helping your aunt with her enquiries.

Pause.

Has she got a boyfriend?

LUKE. I dunno. There's this graffiti in the toilets about how she gave Ludovic Raas chlamydia but. I don't know.

JENNY *has finished cleaning him up. He hides his face in his hands, moans.* JENNY *takes out a small bottle.*

JENNY. Here. Put your tongue out.

LUKE. What is it?

JENNY. Rescue Remedy. Calm you down.

He cautiously sticks his tongue out. She drops a drop on to it. Then unscrews the lid, takes a swig from the bottle herself. Pause.

LUKE. She's basically the only person in the whole school who isn't a fucking backbirth. That place is a fucking zoo. I hate it.

JENNY. Should tell your mum. Get her to move you.

LUKE. I have told her. I tell her constantly, she doesn't listen to me.

JENNY. Well you have to make her.

LUKE. I can't make her. How do I make her?

JENNY. She doesn't take you seriously, that's your problem. She doesn't see you as an actual person.

Pause.

You don't have to tell me anything. We can just sit here or.

Pause.

LUKE. It's so stupid. It's not even.

JENNY. What?

LUKE. I put a leaflet in Natalie's locker

JENNY. Right

LUKE. about HPV

JENNY. okay.

LUKE. it's this STD thing. Virus. It affects your like... cervix, I was in the nurse's office and they had these leaflets about this injection girls can get, which stops you getting it? And I thought she should know so she could, you know. Protect herself.

But so at lunchtime, she comes up to me with Heloise and Stefan and the others and she's like, did you put this in my locker? And they all start laughing. Shouting, throwing stuff, leaves and cans and then Stefan shoves me so I shove him back and he shoves me again and I fall over, and the others are *screaming* with laughter and but Natalie wasn't. She tried to stop him but. He's hitting me, right? Smacking me round the, and because then I saw this big like a stick and I managed to pick it up and I.

JENNY *makes a small noise. She is sitting very still.*

Yeah, and then there's just. Blood. All down his face. All down his shirt. Off his chin and. He's crying. Like, openly crying. In front of everyone, and the girls are, so I just ran.

Pause.

They laugh at everything. They laugh like *constantly*, like everything's funny, and I watch them, and in my head I'm thinking about how they're going to die. Not in a threatening way not like *planning* it, just… statistically. You know.

,

You know?

Pause.

JENNY. Grow up, Luke.

He looks at her. Blindsided.

LUKE. What?

JENNY. Seriously, sort yourself out. All this? Over what? A leaflet? This poor girl. Natalie, is it? She's walking around, what is she, your age? Seventeen, is she pretty?

LUKE. Yes. But

JENNY. Course she is, pretty, happy, lots of mates, lovely young cervix, sunny day like this, probably off the park after school, shopping centre, have a… slush puppie or whatever with her lovely young cervix, and then she opens her locker and there's you. Boom, shitting on her peace of mind with a brand-new horrible fucking thing that might happen to her. Did she ask for that? No. So what you've done there is basically infected her. She's a teenage girl, she's got enough worries, trust me, and there's you dropping another one on her, out of the blue, drive by, here you go love, chew on that.

Lie in bed at night thinking about that, googling that, worrying about that, I mean fair play to her honestly. I'd want to smack you one too.

LUKE. It wasn't her, she didn't, it was / Stefan

JENNY. Because honestly? That's weird. A leaflet, that's objectively just a very weird thing to, and I'm not saying this to be nasty, it's not your fault, what does your mum say, 'be yourself'? Know why she does that? Cos she has no idea what else to say to you. Cos it scares her, you being like this. Cos honestly, you're so like your dad it's not even funny. You are, you're the spit, the stuff comes out your mouth. So there's that, maybe you can't help behaving like a fruit-loop, but if you can, and I would say, you know, have a good go at it, cos if you can, you should knock it on the head sharpish cos otherwise, honestly, I don't see you having a very happy life. Sweetheart.

,

That's it, that's me done. I'm only saying this to help you, let's forget about it now. Have a cup of tea.

She lights a cigarette.

LUKE. Go outside! You want to smoke, go outside, it's not rocket science.

JENNY. You want to try one? I won't tell.

LUKE *smashes his foot into the sofa.*

LUKE. No I *don't* want to get cancer, *thank you*!

JENNY. You're showing off now. Give me a hug

LUKE. Um, no thanks. I don't / think so

JENNY. suit yourself.

LUKE. don't think I want a hug with a murderer actually.

,

Sorry. I didn't. That came out

JENNY. No. Glad. Thanks. Thank you. Actually. Does my head in, Mum and Alice acting like, why can't they say it?

The social worker, she basically said it, why can't any of
you, walking round like I've got BO and no one wants to
tell me. What are they afraid of?

LUKE. Really?

JENNY. Yeah.

LUKE. I think they're afraid you might kill yourself.

Pause.

JENNY. Is your birthday the 12th or the 22nd?

LUKE. The 22nd.

JENNY *types four digits into* ALICE's *phone, the code works.*

JENNY. Cheers.

THE FEMALE CANCERS

5 p.m. An empty beer garden in Geneva. JENNY *with a beer.*
HENRI *with a water.*

HENRI. Perhaps we should wait inside?

JENNY. She'll see us. She's just held up at work. Probably
unifying the universe as we speak! 'Hurry up Universe! I have
to meet my boyfriend!', I can't get my head round it can you?

HENRI. She is a very extraordinary woman. What they
achieved today. Incroyable. You must be very proud of her.

JENNY *shrugs. A pause.* HENRI *checks his phone.*

JENNY. No but the thing that really gets me is this thing this
Higgs thing.

HENRI. Boson.

JENNY. Yeah cos it's just, it's you know. Hypothesis! Their
ideas didn't work so they invented some particle to solve it
well sorry we can all do that, my marriage isn't working

because we don't have a cappuccino machine I mean fuck off right! And maybe I haven't got a PhD but I help people. You know, and I am good at my job.

HENRI. Sorry, what is your job?

JENNY *laughs*.

JENNY. Alice didn't? Okay. This… is a phone, okay so I'm ringing you.

She hands him an imaginary phone. He takes it, confused.

Briiing briiing it's ringing!

HENRI. Oh, okay – (*Picks up the pretend phone.*) Hello?

JENNY. Hello madam.

HENRI. Oh. (*Higher voice.*) Hello!

JENNY *laughs*.

JENNY. I'm calling today madam to ask if you're concerned about the female cancers? I'm talking here about breast cancer, ovarian cancer, vaginal cancer. Did you know madam, you're likely to contract one of these cancers in your lifetime? And if that does happen, have you considered the effect it may have on your income and your ability to keep up loan repayments?

HENRI (*high voice*). Do you have a cure?

JENNY. No. But for just ten pounds a month, you can rest safe in the knowledge that when cancer strikes, you'll be provided for by our unique FemPlan Policy. Is that something you'd be interested in?

HENRI (*high voice*). Oh, yes.

JENNY. That's great madam, thanks for giving me your valuable time today. If you stay on the line, one of my colleagues will take your details.

JENNY hangs up her pretend phone. HENRI follows.

See. I just sold a man insurance against vaginal cancer. I'm fucking great at my job. What do you do?

HENRI. Alice didn't?

JENNY. We just call you The Quaker. That's how you met, right?

HENRI. Yes, it was at the Quaker House.

JENNY. I went to one of them once. Was fucking boring. All these people sitting in silence, waiting for something to happen. Left after about two minutes.

HENRI. So you are not a Quaker too?

JENNY. No. Going straight to Hell me. Do not pass Go! Do not collect two hundred pounds! She only became one when she got married, that did my head in too, the scientist who believes in God! Sorry, what did you say you did?

HENRI. I'm a scientist.

JENNY. Taxi!

They laugh.

HENRI. There's a lot of us in Geneva. The odds are against you. I work for the World Health Organisation. I'm a research entomologist, I develop insecticides. Avicides, bactericides, organophosphates, miticides, virucides, obviously and the new kid on the block, paldoxins. Very exciting the paldoxin, I'm sorry, this is boring?

JENNY. A bit. No, I'm joking, go on.

HENRI. Okay, so for example, malaria? This is a big problem. The mosquito, the tiny fragile creature you can kill with your thumb, she is responsible for more deaths than any other animal. For a time we have good results with DDT. Spray it on crops, spray it on houses. It prevents the disease spreading.

JENNY. Job done.

HENRI. Well, no. Because the young learn, they build resistance.

JENNY. The young are stronger.

HENRI. Eventually the insecticides stop working.

JENNY. Got to kill the old instead. The old are a danger. The old are in the grip of fear. Every year you live you get more afraid.

HENRI. So instead, you target the mosquito at the point in its life cycle that it actually becomes dangerous. It is beautiful, do you not think?

JENNY. Kill the old and save the young! It's brilliant. It's, that's brilliant.

JENNY *puts a hand on his leg.*

HENRI. Perhaps we should wait inside?

JENNY *takes her hand away. Lights a cigarette.*

JENNY. Listen, what about the poor old mosquito?

HENRI. People are dying. In horrible, painful ways people are dying in Africa, and India.

JENNY. Yeah but there's loads of them to start with.

HENRI. Loads of what?

JENNY. Africans. And Indians. We live on an overpopulated planet.

HENRI. Sorry, what is your...?

JENNY. What I'm saying is, you lose a few here, lose a few there... is that really a bad thing, like... statistically?

HENRI. That is a very brutal... I find what you say very offensive.

JENNY. Okay. And you're not scared of some poor brown people dying. You're scared of not having a purpose. Of being, obsolescent.

HENRI. Obsolescent?

JENNY. You're bad as fucking plumbers, just making work for yourself. What are they spending on this collider thing, six million euros?

HENRI. Billion.

JENNY. Fuck off. Six billion? For something that you can't see and might not be there in the first place? Okay so there you go. Tons of stuff you could do with six billion euros. You're so worried about *Africans*, give *them* six billion euros, / bet they'd

HENRI. The work we are doing will improve the lives / of

JENNY. Yeah but it's like when your gran gives you a birthday present isn't it, you'd rather just have the cash

HENRI. Alice is very late.

JENNY. fucking scientists! Listen, I met this woman. Back home, in England

HENRI. I hope something has not happened to her.

JENNY. ah, that's nice. Anyway, this woman had a little girl, and one day, when the girl was a baby, this woman reads this story. In the paper. And it says that a scientist has discovered that this vaccine, this INJECTION, the same injection that her little girl is due to have the very next week, he says that this injection is a DANGER. That could cause the BRAIN of their little girl to go wrong. You know. Go a bit *Rain Man*. A bit special bus. A bit, like if they made a film of her life, the actress that played her would definitely get an Oscar.

And on the one hand, that might make her a musical genius.

But on the other hand they haven't got a piano.

,

HENRI. Jenny, I know, you don't have / to

JENNY. No but wait, this is the good bit, but so this woman Puts Her Foot Down. She Puts Her Foot Down hard, says no way is my girl getting that shit pumped into her. Which is weird cos she's quite a nervous sort – only she had the fear in her see. And the fear made her strong.

And so the little girl never gets that injection.

And eighteen months later the woman finds her little girl is covered in red spots. And the spots are followed by pneumonia, and the pneumonia is followed by a coma and the coma is followed by

followed by this, her mother, meeting me in a bar a bit worse for wear and also having taken smoking up again in quite a big way, and I say to her, no offence but you look like shit sweetheart.

and she says my heart is broken and I want to die.

and I say I'm sorry to hear that. How can I help?

and she says you can't help. Because it's done, I did it and I can never undo it. And I tell her not to be daft because it wasn't, it wasn't just her fault, and she says okay. Okay well if you get the scientist who wrote the report, and you get all the journalists who reported the report, and if you get the Prime Minister, who said the report was right, and if you get all the women on the internet who went on like they knew what they were talking about, even though they knew fuck all, if you get all those people, and put them against a wall, and shoot them in the head one by one then, then I might not feel so fucking lonely for a fucking minute.

Measles Mumps and Rubella. Sounds like a pack of lawyers doesn't it?

Pause.

HENRI. Jenny, it is so kind of you to wait with / me but

JENNY. What, am I boring you! I am, I'm boring you to death aren't I! S'alright, bore myself most of the time

HENRI. Alice is coming soon?

JENNY. no. I don't think so. I found her mobile, I sent the text. We had a fight. I won't speak to her until she apologises.

HENRI. For what?

JENNY. Have you been listening to anything I've said?

JENNY *takes off her sweater. She wears a low-cut top.*
HENRI *looks at her.*

HENRI. Why did you want to meet me?

JENNY. I want her to feel stupid. I want something to happen to her that she'll never be able to understand.

HENRI. Her husband walked out on her. He disappeared. But you still have a husband, I think? So there you are. You win.

JENNY. Mike left, he's staying with his mother. *Irene.* Fucking poison in a tracksuit, wouldn't talk to me at the funeral.

She's done a number on Mike, I tell you. He said he's going to sue me. I don't think he can do that, can he?

HENRI. I don't think so, no.

JENNY. I don't care. I'm not going home. I'm going on holiday. Somewhere hot where they serve English food. Mike always made us go to Scotland. Bird-watching. Fucking pac-a-macs and thirteen hours in a car.

HENRI. Jenny.

JENNY. We saw an eagle once, that was good. Mike started crying he was so happy. Dick.

HENRI. This is not healthy behaviour.

JENNY. When eagles have two chicks, the older one terrorises the younger one until it dies of its wounds.

HENRI. You should not have brought me here like this, Alice / will be

JENNY. I'm a weak force. She's a strong one. She finds everything easy and I find everything hard. I hate her.

JENNY *kisses* HENRI. HENRI *pushes her off.*

HENRI. I definitely think I will go now.

JENNY *kisses him again, he pushes her away, harder.*

Stop it, you don't want this.

JENNY. We don't have to tell her.

HENRI. But I think that you would. I think the point would be to tell her.

JENNY. Yes, probably. I'm not wearing any pants.

HENRI. Neither am I.

JENNY. Shut up.

HENRI. I have a yeast infection. My testicles have to breathe.

JENNY. That's disgusting. Shall we go to a hotel or to your place?

HENRI. Does this usually work?

JENNY. Yes.

HENRI. Really?

JENNY. Englishmen aren't very complicated.

HENRI. Well, I am Swiss. I must go now.

JENNY. Where? To one of your 'meetings'?

HENRI. Probably, yes.

JENNY. Alice told me.

HENRI. It isn't a secret, it isn't a shame –

JENNY. Should be. You're French aren't you?

HENRI. No, I am Swiss.

JENNY. Imagine being French and not allowed a drink.

HENRI. *I am Swiss.*

JENNY. Can't you just have a little one? Let's go back to yours and have a little one.

   JENNY *reaches for his crotch,* HENRI *bats her hand away.*

HENRI. No Jenny, let's go inside and make love there, on the floor of the bar, and other men will hold you down and take a turn and then because at last the dreadful thing you have waited for your whole life will finally have happened, you will at last be happy.

JENNY. I already have that *thing*, my daughter is dead you fucking prick.

HENRI. Yes but that was *your* fault not the universe's!

   HENRI *exits. As* JENNY *talks she takes out a bottle of paracetemol and shakes a handful out. Takes them with her beer.*

JENNY. I'll tell her anyway. I'll say you rang the house and asked to meet me and touched my leg and told me I was more beautiful and she'll cry and I and I, I'll make her tea and we'll talk about how shit you all are, men, how much the same and and and after we'll be stronger, we'll be a fucking fortress and you you you you'll never get in again because

we're blood, we're blood, and you're just some guy with
yeast on his balls.

She shakes out another handful, begins to take these. HENRI
returns. Gathered.

HENRI. Jenny. I should not have spoken like this. This is

Jenny. I would like to apologise. I was

He sees the pills. The effort with which she is swallowing.

what / are you

JENNY. It's okay. Don't, because honestly / it's okay

*He moves towards her, alarmed, she crams more pills into
her mouth, swallows them.*

HENRI. You are not serious? This is, no. It is a joke, yes?

JENNY *shakes her head, takes a drink of beer, struggling to
swallow the pills.*

C'est une blague, you are a soap opera! This is not a real,
this is not what a real person does! No, I – no, this is, you
are monstrous.

What did you take? What / did you take?

JENNY. it doesn't matter

She reaches for the pills again.

HENRI. Stop it!

He grabs the bottle.

Mais elle est malade.

JENNY. yeah, I know, sorry.

HENRI *takes out his phone, dials.*

HENRI. Is okay, I call the ambulance –

JENNY. Yeah, I'm really sorry, but don't, / don't do that

JENNY *grabs his phone and drops it in the glass of water.*

HENRI. Jenny! Putain, mais quel conne!

JENNY. Don't call anyone, I don't want anyone called.

HENRI *runs off, shouting.*

Au secours! Lâche-moi! mon amie fait une tentative de suicide, appelez les secours! Lâche-moi!

HENRI *returns.*

Will you just hold my hand? Please, because I'll just go to sleep in a bit.

She drinks from the carafe.

HENRI. What? No! No, no, no, no, no, no hors de question, we take you to the hospital!

JENNY *grabs at him again.*

Let go. Let go!

JENNY. Please though.

HENRI *wrenches himself free.*

HENRI. Your disease is not terminal, Jenny. Je reviens tout de suite, je reviens!

HENRI *runs out.*

JENNY. Honestly. It's alright. Please. I do know, I do realise this is a really horrible thing to do to you. I do feel bad about it but you must be able to understand Henri. I think if you were really honest you'd understand, because logically, I mean scientifically

this is just. Darwin. Isn't it?

Sudden black.

JENNY'S HERE

ALICE*'s house. Later.* ALICE *on the phone, pacing in the background.* HENRI *watching* ALICE. KAREN *watching* HENRI.

KAREN. I had relations with a Frenchman once. In Cambridge. He drove a mobile cheese van door to door.

HENRI. This is after Alice's father died?

KAREN. Alice's father was sticking his carbon nanotube into every female research assistant on the rota. Wasn't a week went by I didn't find some pudding in a pencil skirt trying to roll down her girdle in a hurry.

ALICE *enters, on the phone.*

ALICE....Oui... oui... non, il a dix-sept ans...

HENRI *gets up to go to* ALICE.

KAREN. I'm not dried up. I am not some fleshless nothing.

ALICE....il y a environ cinq heures... Je sais mais... Oui je le sais... il a eu un problème, a l'école et... oui mais il est vingt-deux heures...

KAREN. I have always had a healthy interest in intercourse.

HENRI. But of course.

KAREN. I could still menstruate if I felt inclined.

ALICE. oui... oui, je comprends... oui. Oui, merci. Au revoir.

ALICE *hangs up.*

HENRI. What did they say?

ALICE. They won't do anything. We have to wait twenty-four hours before they'll even register him as missing. What did you want to tell me?

HENRI. It can wait. Sit. Breathe now, I make you some coffee.

HENRI *goes out.*

ALICE. Luke it's me again. I'm sorry, I just, we're all very, we're sitting up here and it's very late. I'm sure you're, I'm sure you are but. I love you.

As ALICE *talks,* KAREN *tries to reach the bathroom but wets herself. She is embarrassed, and tries to clean it up without being seen by* ALICE. JENNY *enters, unkempt, in* HENRI's *coat.*

KAREN. Jenny.

JENNY. It's okay.

ALICE. Oh Mum…

KAREN *whispers in* JENNY's *ear.*

JENNY. It's alright. Go and get changed.

ALICE. For God's sakes…

KAREN. Grow up Alice. Only a bit of piss.

KAREN *exits.* JENNY *quickly cleans up the urine.*

ALICE. She did that in the control room today. Had to tie my jacket round her waist.

JENNY. It happens.

ALICE. I thought it was the excitement. Have you taken her to the doctor?

JENNY. No, I thought I'd use my magic crystals to heal her. Why, do you think it's not working?

ALICE *lets out a deep breath.*

I've tried to take her. She won't go.

ALICE. Why not?

JENNY. Dunno. You know what she's like.

ALICE. Well you have to make her.

JENNY. Do I? You know *you* can be there if you want

ALICE. You know I would, but

JENNY. but you think your work's more important

ALICE. what?

JENNY. can't stand to be near us, minute you finished your degree you were on a plane to Massachusetts.

ALICE. For my PhD, sorry can we not, / right now because

JENNY. England has PhDs too, and don't, that's not, because the moment you finished that you came over here.

ALICE. I was in love.

JENNY. With a fucking headcase.

ALICE *starts to cry.*

Yeah that's it. Cry. That's really helpful. You're only doing it so Mum'll come in and take your side.

ALICE. I'm forty-three!

JENNY. I'm not crying. I buried my daughter six weeks ago I'm not crying.

HENRI *runs in, sees* JENNY. *Sees* ALICE's *distress.*

HENRI. What are you doing here? What did she say?

ALICE. Why's she wearing your coat?

JENNY *takes off the coat. Underneath there is a large black stain down her clothes.*

HENRI. We have more than your problems to deal with, yes? Luke is missing.

JENNY. What?

ALICE. He didn't come back here? You didn't see him?

JENNY. No.

ALICE. No, just because, you were here all day, you're sure you didn't?

,

Jen? Please, / because

JENNY. Yeah. I mean. No, I'm sure I didn't

KAREN *enters.*

ALICE. You're sure? You have to think, because I'm just trying to work out what could've happened, to make him react / like

JENNY. I didn't see him. I wasn't here. I went to the Jardin Anglais.

ALICE. Did you?

JENNY. Yeah and then I was with Henri, / so

ALICE. Why were you with Henri?

KAREN. Are we thinking it's drugs?

ALICE. No we are not thinking that – (*To* HENRI.) what is she talking about?

KAREN. He's a teenager dear.

ALICE. He doesn't even drink, can someone / please explain?

KAREN. If he did he wouldn't tell you. He thinks his father is working for some sort of secret *agency*, did you know that?

JENNY. Mum, / stop it.

ALICE. Henri?

HENRI. It is her business to tell you, not mine.

KAREN. I think he might be slightly unusual.

JENNY. Go to bed Mum!

KAREN. You see Henri? You see how I'm treated by these girls, it's degrading, you wouldn't do it to a dog.

HENRI *laughs, hollow. Turns to* KAREN, *with chivalry.*

HENRI. But it's late, no? We are all upset. Come, go and sit down, I will bring you some tea.

KAREN. Some civility! At last, yes, thank you Henri, it takes a Frenchman doesn't it? It seems it takes a Frenchman!

HENRI *ushers* KAREN *out of the room. When she is gone, to* JENNY:

HENRI. You owe me fifty Francs, okay! For the ambulance and also for my coat, for the dry cleaning, okay? / I am so serious, I will not pay for the honour of watching you masturbate, I will not pay for this!

ALICE. What? Could someone please

HENRI. She calls me to a bar to give me some big theatre show,
she takes pills, she wants me to sit with her, she wants an
audience yes? She wants an audience to tell her speech to,
she wets my phone, she scares the shit from me, she... I hold
her hand in the ambulance, I tell her of my dark times, to
comfort her... this is a personal okay? A precious, but I tell it
to her, then I take her to the hospital and all the way she
screams at me that I will go to Hell.

HENRI *is nearly in tears but they are now subsumed by rage
again.*

Insupportable! Insupportable!

(*To* ALICE.) I used to think the only unkind thing about you
was the way you talked of your sister. Now I know what a
nice portrait you make of her, I mean this, I mean this
absolutely, there is something wrong with you

ALICE. *Henri

HENRI. *in your brain, and I am sorry for your sadness Jenny
but when I look at you, I don't see a woman, I see a terrible
thing, a toxic thing like a cloud like a gas a black gas and it
affects all of us you know, that's what – you affect us too
okay! That's what you must understand! You affect all of us!

ALICE. Okay, I think you should leave.

HENRI. You think that I...?

ALICE. Yes, I think you've been drinking and it would be
better for you / and for all of us actually if you went home.

HENRI. I haven't been drinking. I haven't been drinking, one
mouth of a beer! One mouth of a beer because of her,
because *she* –

ALICE. She's lost her *daughter*, please, just go.

HENRI *tries to touch* ALICE.

HENRI. Alice, please –

ALICE. No. You don't speak to her like that, I'm sorry but you
do not speak to her / like that.

HENRI. Fine. Fine, I take to your mother her tea and then I go home to be sane. The pair of you... the pair of you.

HENRI snatches his coat, exits. Pause. ALICE looks at JENNY.

JENNY. It's not his fault.

ALICE. I know it's not his fault!

JENNY. I asked him not to tell you.

ALICE. Why?

JENNY. I dunno. I tried to fuck him.

ALICE. Well that's not

JENNY. I know

ALICE. that's not okay!

JENNY. no, I know, I do regret that.

ALICE. well are you are you are you alright?

JENNY. I'm okay. They made me drink charcoal. Like a drink made of charcoal, was disgusting.

Then I found out it was gonna cost me two hundred Francs to stay the night in hospital. I said, what happens next? They said, you'll throw up. I said, right, well I can do that for nothing at home.

So I called a taxi, walked out. Vommed in the car park.

Two hundred Francs. What's wrong with this country?

ALICE is in tears.

Are you cross with me?

ALICE. No, I'm not cross with you.

JENNY. Look at me and say you're not cross with me.

ALICE looks at her.

ALICE. I'm not cross with you.

KAREN enters, distressed, in her nightgown.

KAREN. Where's Henri?

ALICE. He's gone, Mum.

KAREN. He promised me a hot drink.

JENNY. It's in your hand.

> KAREN *looks at the mug. Back at* JENNY.

KAREN. I know what this is about you know. No one tells me anything but I *worked it out*, it's about that poor man.

JENNY. Go to bed, Miss Marple.

KAREN. Do you know what I wish, I wish he'd just killed himself. At least then you could get on with things.

> JENNY *marches over to* KAREN *and knocks the tea out of her hand, vicious.*

> You spilt my tea!

JENNY. You go to bed!

KAREN. My tea that Henri made me!

JENNY. ME AND ALICE ARE TALKING NOW.

KAREN. Shouting at me! I'm not, I should have won a / Nobel Prize!

> JENNY*'s heard this a thousand times, on autopilot.*

JENNY. 'Nobel Prize'.

KAREN. It isn't bloody funny! Your father didn't allow for anomalies, he got that prize for the anomaly I saw! He didn't have the rigour and that's the truth of it but that's effing Cambridge for you, I was just the grammar-school *tart*, even after we were married, the way he spoke to me, 'Karen dear, there is a difference between skipper and crew, even if the cabin boy spots the iceberg' – my God! If it wasn't for the pair of you, my concern you shouldn't come from a broken home, I would have divorced him! Like that!

JENNY. You did divorce him!

KAREN. But at a much later date!

JENNY. This isn't about you!

KAREN. I am the head of this family. My grandson is missing, and you send me to bed, like a child, like an infant, well I won't have it, I want us to have a have a, a, a... an... an

JENNY. Orgy. Scrabble / tournament.

KAREN. mature conversation, stop it. Stop it you stupid girl.

JENNY. I'm not stupid, / don't

KAREN. Yes you are, you're a silly woman. You're a silly, wicked woman.

JENNY. Oh, shut up Mum.

KAREN. You wicked wicked girl!

  KAREN *suddenly yanks* JENNY*'s hand, drags* JENNY *to her.*

JENNY. Alice, help me! Child abuse! She's so strong!

  KAREN *lays* JENNY *across her lap, holds her there. Pulls down* JENNY*'s trousers and knickers and smacks her repeatedly.* JENNY *cannot believe this is happening but refuses to let her mother see any weakness in her.*

KAREN. You stupid stubborn girl!

JENNY. Oh, yeah, little to the left! Come on, put your back / into it!

ALICE. Mum, stop it!

  ALICE *tries to stop* KAREN, KAREN *elbows her away.*

KAREN. Think you're so clever, I told you, I told you, / Mike told you, you don't *listen* you never *listen*

  KAREN *keeps smacking* JENNY. JENNY *tries to rear up, but* KAREN *grabs* JENNY *by the hair and yanks her head down again.* JENNY *cries out in pain.*

  That poor little / creature

ALICE. Mum, stop

JENNY. Allie she's / hurting me

KAREN. Pig-headed and ignorant, you've always / been like it

ALICE. Mum, stop it!

KAREN. that poor little / creature

JENNY. Mum please, please Mum / please Mum

KAREN. poor little sweet little

KAREN *throws* JENNY *from her.*

THAT POOR DEAR SWEET LITTLE THING.

KAREN *exits.* JENNY *staggers to her feet, lurches, retching and suddenly throws up. An eruption of charcoal. An explosion of dark matter. The sound of a black hole.*

ALICE. Jenny? Oh my God. Oh my God, are / you

JENNY *wipes her mouth. Tries to smile.*

JENNY. It's alright. I'm alright.

ALICE *starts to cry. They crawl towards each other, hold each other.*

We're alright. Jenny's here. Jenny's got you. Jenny's got you. Shhh shh shh. Shh shh shh. Shhh shh shhh… Jenny's got you now…

JENNY *kisses* ALICE *on the head. It leaves a black smear, as the Higgs Field appears around them. A shimmering fog. It gets brighter and brighter till it hurts our eyes.* ALICE *and* JENNY *disappear in its intensity.* JENNY*'s 'shhh's turn into static, and then a humming of mosquitoes, that grows and grows, until* THE BOSON *enters with a mop and bucket.*

THE BOSON

The stage is clear except for a puddle of JENNY*'s black bile.*
THE BOSON *starts to mop it up. As his speech goes on, we
become aware his mopping is only making the puddle larger
and larger.*

THE BOSON. There are five ways for the world to end.

Spoiler alert.

One. The Big Crunch. As you know, the universe is
expanding but – sorry am I going too fast?

Fine, in case you didn't know: the universe is expanding (why
didn't you know that? seriously, read a book some time) but
anyway let's say that the elastic snaps the worm turns and
eventually it begins to *contract*, getting smaller hotter denser,
a double decker wrapper in the microwave, till it's basically
just a, just a very compact inferno, so that's one, okay, two, the
Big Freeze, does what it says on the, HEAT DEATH,
everything becomes same temperature, the universe is now
uniformly cold, dead and empty and nothing interesting ever
happens again, number three, the Big Change, dark energy
keeps growing, pulling the universe apart, till one day a
bubble of lower energy shows up, expands at the speed of
light, rewriting the rules of chemistry and destroying humans,
planets, stars, et cetera, in at number four, if the amount of
dark energy increases too fast we might get a Big Rip, which
is, you know, pretty much what it, have you seen *Star Trek*?
kind of like that, atoms shatter and the Earth (understandably)
explodes, and by the way no offence, no offence, but it's
unlikely that any of you are able to understand any of this in
except in the most rudimentary terms. Most of you probably
don't even know whether any of this is true or not

*He pauses. Shields his eyes, scrutinising the front few rows,
double-checking.*

yeah. No. That's okay. That's okay. You're doing your best,
and the thing is, it *feels* true doesn't it? The idea that all of this
will end in a catastrophe over which we have no power, that's
a given, that is a familiar and strangely comforting fact, be it
fire, ice, cosmic menopause, atomic obliteration, or a

contagion perhaps, a virus spreading too fast for us to control,
an ice floe melting too quickly, a shortage of food,
a war over water, a bad day on the golf course for a sociopath
with access to the nuclear codes, or for example, for example
number five, one day you're at home cooking this soup I mean
not from scratch or anything but you know you got that carton
open so you're feeling pretty fucking pleased with yourself
and as it starts to bubble you become aware your blood has
been replaced by battery acid and this is, yeah it's a disturbing
thought but it's a familiar one, you've had this thought before,
many times actually but you've always been able to receive it
with a kind of like a healthy skepticism, the way you think
about crop circles or the charitable gestures of millionaires and
but what's different today is that you can no longer tell the
difference between this piece of information and any other
piece of information, it arrives in your brain in the same font
as any other *fact*: that is a toaster the kettle is metal you live in
geneva taekwondo is an olympic sport angelica huston speaks
fluent french the human immunodeficiency virus cannot be
spread by mosquitoes anthrax is a disease aeschynite is a
mineral your heart is a pump for battery acid you are cooking
soup for your son your son is eight your son is upstairs in bed
with a cold and that's when you realise somehow the seal of
your body has *broken* and this acid this acid is no longer
contained by your skin veins arteries flesh it's leaching
through the pads of your fingers it's in your saliva the moisture
in your eyes sweat on your back neck a wetness a taste in your
burning corroding contaminating everything you black smears
on the spoon on the bowl you've put on a tray to take to your
son who is eight who is upstairs in bed with a cold with a
temperature with a fever caused by a rot and suddenly you
understand you are the rot you are the disease and then there is
a sound like a click like the click of a catch of suitcase and
there is relief there is relief because there is order now,
whatever else, there is order and so you turn off the gas and
leaving your coat and your wallet and your mobile phone
behind you, you walk out of the

Sudden black.

Interval.

ACT THREE

THE JARDIN ANGLAIS

Five days later. LUKE, *in the Jardin Anglais, by Lake Geneva. He's on the floor, he's been knocked down, in shock. Behind him, the clock made of flowers.*

NATALIE *stands a way off, screaming at someone, off.*

NATALIE. Fuck off piece of shit fucking kill you! Are you alright? Did he hurt you?

LUKE. Took / my.

NATALIE. What?

LUKE. Took my coat.

NATALIE. Fucking prick. You're alright though?

LUKE. What do you want Natalie?

NATALIE. You could actually be a bit polite you know. I think he had a knife. If I hadn't been / here

LUKE. He didn't have a knife.

NATALIE. No I think he did you know.

LUKE. He didn't.

NATALIE. Sorry but how you could see that curled up on the floor crying?

LUKE. Why are you following me?

NATALIE. 'Scuse me, other way round.

LUKE. No.

NATALIE. Shut up, no, I saw you. Outside Celeste's. Outside school.

LUKE. Wasn't me.

NATALIE. Weird. Looked a lot like you. This person. So after school I followed This Person and This Person came here to the Jardin Anglais, and then This Person got like, *assaulted* and I like, rescued him, so unless this is like a parallel universe you are That Person so don't even like bother lying to me okay? By the way I'm not being nasty but you stink.

Pause.

Where've you been?

LUKE. This lorry driver picked me up. Drove me to Frankfurt. Then another one took me to Ravensbrück

NATALIE. Shut up.

LUKE. Yeah it was, it was… frightening, I got a bus back to Berlin then a train then another train, took for ever. Germany's really big, which I mean I knew that before but only like, theoretically.

NATALIE. Where've you been sleeping? Have you been sleeping here?

LUKE. Yeah.

NATALIE. Weren't you cold?

LUKE. Yeah.

NATALIE. Weren't you scared?

LUKE. Yeah.

NATALIE. What's Germany like?

LUKE. Like here pretty much. Boring.

NATALIE. You said it was frightening.

LUKE. It was, it's boring and frightening. Like here. Like everywhere.

NATALIE. Your mum's been at school every day with the police and some mental woman who shouts at everyone.

LUKE. My Aunt Jenny.

NATALIE. There's pictures of you on all the bus stops. Why d'you come back? I'd never come back. I'd just keep going.

LUKE. I didn't want to get you into trouble.

NATALIE. You already did. You already did get me into trouble. Your mum's a bitch, she made them look at all the CCTV. Tried to blame it on Stefan, she got him suspended from college, and, everyone's acting like it's my fault. They went to the Meyrin Centre on Friday and no one even told me, and when I asked Heloise about it she was like, I don't why you're acting all Mother Teresa now, you started all this, you know you're going to Hell, don't you Natalie? She's a Catholic so.

But I kept thinking, what if he's dead cos of me and that was something I just have to, like my cousin, he was in the army and he gave this order but the order was wrong and loads of kids got, actually I'm not sposed to talk about it but anyway I kept thinking, if I could just see him, then. Then I could, I'm sorry okay? I'm really sorry and I'm not just saying that so I don't go to Hell.

,

LUKE. I think some people shouldn't be allowed to have kids, don't you?

NATALIE. Yes I do actually. I think there's lots of people at our school which, if you sterilised them, then in fifty years' time the world would just be like a much better place but you're not sposed to say that are you?

LUKE. I'm not going home till she's gone.

,

NATALIE. Okay, well. Your skin's like blue? You look really cold.

LUKE. I am.

NATALIE. You look really sad.

LUKE. Yeah.

,

NATALIE. Think you should come home with me.

TECHNOLOGY

ALICE *at home in her pyjamas, a coat over them. She has not washed or brushed her hair for some days.* JENNY *has a magazine.*

ALICE. I don't know.

JENNY. You do though.

ALICE. I don't know.

JENNY. As if you don't, everyone knows / their

ALICE. I don't

JENNY. You do!

ALICE. Okay well then I don't care.

JENNY. Okay well I don't care either.

>   ,

>   I'm just trying to help.

>   ,

>   Take your mind / off

ALICE. Fine well just pick me a good one and read it out.

JENNY. It doesn't work like that.

ALICE. There isn't a way it works. It isn't a real thing so there isn't 'a / way it works'

JENNY. Are you Leo or Virgo?

ALICE. I don't know

JENNY. Okay well you're the end of the month so you're / probably

ALICE. I think I'm a Capricorn.

JENNY. Your birthday's in August so / that's not

ALICE. So what?

JENNY. so you're not a Capricorn.

ALICE. It's fiction, I can be anything I want, I can be a Hufflepuff if I want, I want to be a Capricorn.

JENNY. Fine. Fuck it. Let's all be a Capricorn.

,

ALICE. Go on then.

JENNY. No, it won't mean anything.

Pause.

Do you want to take the coat off, / or?

ALICE. Just go to bed.

JENNY. I'm not leaving you on your own. I'm just trying to help.

ALICE. Do you know where my son is?

,

Jen do you know where Luke is?

,

JENNY. Don't think the worst. You don't know.

ALICE. Yes I do. I do know. I've done this before. I can predict the future, this is what's going to happen: tomorrow the police will suggest we drag the lake which, I'll watch them and it'll take a long time, because Lake Geneva is a very big lake, and people like to dump old carpets in it so every couple of hours they'll find one of these carpets and start hauling it out and every single one of those carpets will look like a body.

And then I'll spend five hundred Francs on photocopying and travel to various European cities to hand out these photocopies to people and some of them, the ones who actually, they'll stare at his face for a few minutes and then forget it completely, and then I'll come back here and I'll wait, and I'll wait and eventually, I mean after years, the worst possible outcome will become the best because because at least then at least then...

Pause.

JENNY. Do you still think about him?

ALICE. Of course. Of course I still. Sometimes I feel like he's. Or I look at Luke and. Or, last year, there was a fire, they found a body, an English man with dark hair it was on the news / and

JENNY. But it wasn't him

ALICE. No of course it wasn't him. Of course it wasn't but still there's always a moment when your stomach flips over and.

,

And but or sometimes. Whenever I feel sort of.
Overwhelmed and. By fear, I mean, or. Terror, what, well, saves me is I feel his hand on the back of my neck, and he just, he squeezes it.

She demonstrates on JENNY.

Like that. That's all.

Pause.

JENNY. By the way I never told you.

ALICE. What?

JENNY. I meant to tell you, Mike tried to get me arrested.

ALICE. No.

JENNY. Yeah, after, like the day after she, he rang the police, these two lads came round, about twelve, could smell the Lynx before they got out the car and I dunno what he'd told them but I think they thought they were gonna find like Miss Hannigan or something, toddlers under the bed but it was just me in my nightie trying to pick a coffin.

,

ALICE. That's awful.

JENNY. No cos actually I felt relieved, actually. First thing that'd happened for ages that made sense to me. Kept trying to get in their car.

Pause.

ALICE. I've never told you this before but I really think Mike's a cunt.

JENNY. Yeah.

ALICE. I've thought it for about twelve years.

Will you pray with me?

JENNY. Oh. No I don't. I mean I don't really believe in it / so

ALICE. Please.

Please.

,

JENNY. What do I, what do we do?

ALICE *closes her eyes.* JENNY *copies, uncertain.*

ALICE. You just wait.

They pray for a few moments.

JENNY *opens her eyes.*

JENNY. Don't we have to say something or, from the Bible / or

ALICE. There's no Bible. You just make it up for yourself.

JENNY *closes her eyes again. They pray in silence.*

A long time.

JENNY. Did you do this when Amy was sick?

ALICE. Yes.

Pause.

JENNY. Thank you.

'Five Years' by David Bowie starts to play.

ALARM

NATALIE, *in her room. Some speakers, the music coming from them. She takes the half-drunk bottle of Crème de Menthe from a pocket on the side of* LUKE*'s bag.* LUKE *enters. He's had a shower. He's dressed again, drying his hair with a towel.*

LUKE. Your shower's amazing. It's like the whitest room I've ever seen.

NATALIE. Think it looks like a gas chamber.

He gestures to the Crème de Menthe.

LUKE. Stole it from my auntie. It's really horrible.

NATALIE. I stole some whiskey from my dad when we lived in New York, topped it up with apple juice but he found out and went mental so I blamed it on the cleaning lady.

LUKE. That's a horrible thing to do.

NATALIE. I know, I felt really bad she was Puerto Rican.

They take it in turns to drink from the bottle.

S'alright. Minty.

She sits, accidentally setting off a personal alarm in her pocket. A piercing shriek.

Oh my God, shut up!

She fumbles for it, turns it off. Smiles at LUKE, *embarrassed.*

Sorry. Rape alarm. My dad makes me carry it. Hate it. He thinks his only job is to make me afraid of stuff. Don't take drugs, your brain will swell don't drink you'll get blisters on your liver don't wear short skirts you'll get raped.

LUKE. Well. Sensible.

NATALIE. He's got no joy. Is your dad like that?

LUKE. My dad doesn't live with us.

NATALIE. Oh yeah the agency thing / right? I forgot, that's

LUKE. Yeah it's like classified.

NATALIE. so random. You gonna sit down or?

He sits. Long pause.

LUKE. Do you have chlamydia?

NATALIE. What. *What?*

LUKE. Sorry.

NATALIE. No I don't have chlamydia! Jesus…

Pause. She drinks.

You can't get it from kissing can you?

LUKE. I don't think so.

NATALIE *takes out her phone. Googles this. Is reassured. Puts her phone away.*

NATALIE. I've only kissed twelve people anyway. So pathetic, right?

LUKE. No. Not. Did you know, neurologically speaking, women are completely emotionless at the point of orgasm? Must be amazing just to be, for your mind to be, blank for half an hour or whatever

NATALIE *laughs. He laughs too. Pause. She moves half a foot closer to him.*

NATALIE. You know all that stuff about your dad?

LUKE. Yeah.

NATALIE. All that stuff yeah, you don't really believe that do you?

,

LUKE. No.

NATALIE. Just it's not very attractive, like it's a bit immature? Cos my mum *left*, she met this guy at a Snow Patrol concert and that's like shit but people leave, don't they? That's just something people do, isn't it?

Pause.

LUKE. He was ill. Mentally, he was mentally ill.

,

NATALIE. Well there you go. Is it like hereditary?

LUKE. I don't know.

NATALIE. Does that freak you out?

LUKE. Yeah it does actually.

NATALIE. Yeah it would freak me out too.

Pause.

This house is built over the Collider. They had to get permission from like two thousand people to drill under their houses. The pipe's running right under us now. Beams of light, or not light is it but

LUKE. Protons.

NATALIE. Einstein.

LUKE. My mum.

NATALIE. Must be amazing. I'm not clever enough to do a job like that. I'm probably just gonna end up being like a doctor or a lawyer can I ask you a question? Your mum doesn't shave her armpits.

,

LUKE. What's the question?

NATALIE. No just it's really disgusting. Anyway that's why Heloise put that razor in your locker, did you get that?

LUKE. No.

NATALIE. Yeah I thought it was a bit fucking oblique. Heloise is so random!

LUKE. She says it's her body.

NATALIE. Yeah but we have to look at it.

NATALIE *takes a long drink of Crème de Menthe.*

You know how people hate you cos you're clever?

LUKE. Okay.

NATALIE. I think that's why people are afraid of scientists. Cos it's like power, isn't it. It's like when Heloise and Celeste speak really fast in German when I'm standing right there. Makes me nervous.

LUKE. Do you want to hear it?

NATALIE. What?

LUKE. The Higgs.

NATALIE. You can't hear it. It's just numbers and graphs and shit.

LUKE. No, this is brilliant actually, because you can use the ATLAS software to process the data which, you can make an algorithm which – you can listen to it, to the sound of the Higgs decaying. You can hear what's happening under your house.

NATALIE. Like a song?

LUKE. At first it's just sounds, but I've. It's not even any good but I can. If you want.

LUKE takes his laptop out, starts it up. NATALIE *turns off the Bowie. He plugs in headphones,* NATALIE *puts them on.* LUKE *plays the track. Only she can hear it. She closes her eyes and listens.* LUKE *watches her.*

She takes the headphones off.

This is just, it's not finished properly / and

NATALIE. I don't really get it.

I mean I'm sure it's good but, I'm just… not clever enough / to

LUKE. Don't say that. Why d'you keep saying that? Just cos everyone you hang around with's thick as shit doesn't / mean

NATALIE. Okay well you're talking about my friends now so

LUKE. Okay well your friends are stupid. And a bit racist, actually. And Heloise told everyone you had pubic shorts.

NATALIE. What?

LUKE. It's like when your pubic / hair

NATALIE. I know what it is.

Long pause. NATALIE *drinks.*

They're not racist. They just.

,

I've never even been to India, so.

Pause. She checks her phone. Puts it down. Checks it again. Puts it down.

So do you wanna have sex or what?

LUKE. Yes. I mean… yes. I mean… yes. I mean yes only

NATALIE. It's fine if you don't fancy me

LUKE. No I do. I do but. It just seems like / quite a

NATALIE. oh my / God this is so awkward.

LUKE. quite a sudden, yeah, sorry.

NATALIE. We don't have to like touch each other or anything.

LUKE. Sure. What?

NATALIE. Like, you stand there and I'll stand like far apart and we can just like, have you got an iPhone?

LUKE. Yeah.

NATALIE. Okay cool cos I did it with Celeste once? It was really hot but then she went properly weird about it and told everyone I was a lesbian even though it was her idea in the first place, what d'you think, does that sound?

LUKE. It sounds weird.

,

I mean I don't see the point.

,

Shall I stand here?

NATALIE. Bit further away.

They stand far apart. NATALIE *strips down to her top and pants. She finishes, looks up at him, makes a face: 'go on then'.* LUKE *strips down to his pants.*

Pause. They look at each other.

NATALIE *takes her bra off under her top, puts her phone under it and takes a picture of her breasts. She sends him the picture. Pause.*

You gonna look at it or?

He takes out his phone.

LUKE. Right, yeah... just have to turn it on.

NATALIE. Who turns their phone off?

LUKE. So they couldn't triangulate my location through the cell towers.

NATALIE. Wow. You're like an evil genius.

LUKE. Thanks.

Pause. The phone is on now. It dings. He looks at it. Breathes.

,

NATALIE. Okay, delete it.

LUKE. Right, yeah.

LUKE *deletes it.*

NATALIE. Did you?

LUKE. Yeah.

NATALIE. 'Kay. Now you.

LUKE. Like...?

NATALIE. Like, stop being a virgin and put your phone down your fucking pants Luke.

Awkward, LUKE *pulls out his waistband, puts his phone down his pants. Takes a picture. The flash goes off. He sends it. Her phone dings. She looks at it. Smiles. Her thumbs start flying.*

LUKE. Are you deleting it?

NATALIE. Yeah yeah yeah.

Pause. Her thumbs keep flying.

LUKE. Natalie.

NATALIE. What?

LUKE. Delete it.

NATALIE. I am.

LUKE. No you're not.

NATALIE. I am! Just give me a –

LUKE. No, delete it. Delete it now.

LUKE *grabs at the phone, she moves it out of the way.*

NATALIE. Oh my God! Fucking, calm down.

LUKE. What are you doing?

NATALIE. Oh my God *calm down*. It's just a joke.

LUKE. What is?

NATALIE. I'm sorry okay but you need to think about how you / affect people

LUKE. What've you done?

NATALIE. cos I'm not being funny but you really embarrassed me and you hurt Stefan. You really hurt him.

She puts her phone away. LUKE*'s phone pings.*

LUKE. What? I don't... what's happening? / What is happening?

NATALIE. You broke his nose. He got suspended. He's my best male friend.

LUKE*'s phone pings again. Again. Again. Again. He looks at it. Ping. Drops it like it is toxic. Hyperventilating. Ping.* NATALIE *ignores him, puts on her trousers. Ping.*

You better go. My dad'll be back soon.

Pingpingpingpingpingpingping, LUKE*'s body buckles, he crumples to the floor, folding his arms round his head.*

LUKE. Get rid of it. Get rid of it.

She laughs. The pinging continues.

NATALIE. 'Get rid of it'?

Um, yeah. No.

That's not really how the internet works?

She surveys him, as his phone pings almost continuously now.

THE NUCLEAR STRONG FORCE

JENNY *is brushing* ALICE*'s hair. Throughout the scene she gets the tangles out and plaits it.* KAREN *in a chair, eating a sandwich.* ALICE *is reading aloud from* JENNY*'s magazine.*

ALICE. Venus, the planet of love and beauty, slides into your zone of intuition. When the sun unites with powerful Pluto pull the trigger on a big decision regarding relationships. If it doesn't feel right, move on. Fitness goals will finally stick this month.

Pause.

KAREN. How is Venus the planet of love and beauty? If you went to Venus it would kill you in ten seconds.

JENNY. I think it's more of a / spiritual

KAREN. You'd be instantaneously cremated.

JENNY. Yeah, I don't… that's good about the fitness goals though.

ALICE. Jenny says you won't see the doctor.

KAREN. Jenny is for once correct.

Pause.

ALICE. Okay. Why not?

KAREN. Because there can be no question.

,

ALICE. What's the question?

KAREN. There can be no question over my, my agency.

ALICE. No one's questioning / your

KAREN. You *know* this Alice, what makes a scientist? The
willingness to abandon bad ideas. To look at the data and,
and recognise failures which should not be repeated.

JENNY. What is she talking about? What *data*?

KAREN. I am… forgetting things. The television, I can't follow
it, and there is a loss of… an issue regarding my…

She wrestles for dignity.

I am struggling to be continent.

ALICE. But. That's not unnatural. For a woman of / your

KAREN. I tried to make a white sauce, this is a recipe I, every
week, forty years, off by heart and I. I had to look it up. A pint
of milk, two ounces of butter, ounce-and-a-half of flour, there
you see, now I can, it slips out like my name now but when
I reached for it… ridiculous.

ALICE. I forget things. I forget things all the time, / it doesn't

KAREN. Yes but I haven't got the time to faff around. I have to
act, while I still have control. Because I watched it happen to
Nana Willis, I'm not going in one of those places.

ALICE. This is, I think we're a long way from / that

KAREN. They put you in other women's clothes. I went in one
day, she was wearing a *fleece*. A woman who wore a *hat* her
whole life, never answered the *telephone* without lipstick,
a *fleece*, someone else's tissues in the pocket, it's not *human*.

ALICE. No one's going to make you wear a fleece, Mum.

KAREN. Please don't patronise me. I am not demented, not yet.
And if a doctor diagnoses me then I'm in the system and if
I'm in the system then they won't let me do it.

JENNY. Do what?

ALICE. She means, assisted, you know, in Zurich, / that is not an

JENNY. A clinic? Her grandson's missing, she's talking about
clinics, listen if that's what you want, *I'll* assist you!

KAREN. Stop showing off.

JENNY. This is my theory, people don't really come to Switzerland with the *intention* of killing themselves, they just come for a normal holiday and get driven to it.

KAREN. Are you making a joke? Is this funny to you? Is your mother, decaying, amusing?

JENNY. Why are we even talking about this? Alice tell her.

ALICE. I do think this is very / extreme

JENNY. Your timing's beautiful by the way, really, just, bang-on.

KAREN. I don't have time. There is / no time.

JENNY. Seriously, you are literally the most selfish person / I ever

KAREN. Beg pardon but it's not your decision. I love you Jenny, but I will not be your dependent. I will not have *you* in charge of me.

> KAREN *exits. Pause.* ALICE *looks round at* JENNY. *They laugh.*

ALICE. You're not going to go, are you?

> JENNY *straightens* ALICE*'s head again so she can go on styling it.*

JENNY. We missed our flight so

ALICE. Is it Thursday?

JENNY. didn't want to leave you like this. Thought we could stay till next week, / or

ALICE. Will you?

JENNY. Yeah. Course.

> ,

Stay longer, if you want. Just as, like an experiment.

ALICE. Yeah?

JENNY. Up to you.

ALICE. No, that'd be. That could be good.

JENNY. Just see how we go.

ALICE. Yeah.

,

Or maybe I could come back to England. Get a, teaching
position.

JENNY. You can't come back. You might win a Nobel Prize.

They laugh. JENNY *has finished* ALICE*'s hair, it is now
plaited into pigtails, like a little girl.* ALICE *smells her own
armpit. Makes a sound of disgust.*

I'll run you a bath.

ALICE. *What if he calls?

JENNY. *Do you good, a bath, then I'll answer it.

ALICE. No, I'll get in the shower. Quicker.

ALICE *goes out.*

The sound of the shower running, off. Pause.

LUKE *enters. He has been running.* JENNY *looks at him.*

JENNY. Alice. Alice!

ALICE *runs in, in bra and pants. They should be the same
colour as* NATALIE*'s in the previous scene.* ALICE *looks at*
LUKE*, frozen for a moment. She flies towards him, smacks
him hard across the face, then instantly embraces him, clasps
him to her. Her near-nakedness is uncomfortable for him.
She kisses his head, his face.*

LUKE. Alright Mum. Alright just

She squeezes him too tightly.

hurting me... Alice...

*She releases him but still keeps contact with his body in
some way.*

ALICE. Where have you been?

LUKE (*re:* JENNY). Why is she / still here?

ALICE. why didn't you call me, you could've called / me you
could've

LUKE. I thought she was going today, why is she still here?

ALICE. I thought you were. Where the hell have you been! I'm sorry, I'm so, I can't, I thought you / were.

LUKE. Can you put some clothes on?

,

Can you please put some clothes on, standing there with your vagina hanging / out.

ALICE. No because I want you to tell me what's going on, / because

LUKE. I want to leave Geneva. I don't want to live here any more.

,

ALICE. Right. Okay.

,

Why?

LUKE. Because I don't.

ALICE. Yes but / why

LUKE. Because I hate it.

ALICE. Since when?

LUKE. Since for ever. Since the beginning of time. It's a shithole.

JENNY. Can I just –

LUKE. You don't talk! Shouldn't even be here, don't talk to me / do not fucking talk to me

ALICE. Okay forget about that, forget about Auntie Jenny, this isn't about Auntie Jenny, she won't even be here tomorrow, she'll be back in England, the point is, we're not uprooting our whole… for one silly fight? No, this is your education we're / talking about, yes?

JENNY *lights a cigarette*.

LUKE. You're not listening to me, can you listen to me, *I don't want to live here any more*, put it out. Put it out!

LUKE *looks at* JENNY. *She puts her fag out*.

ALICE. But there's no reason. Give me / a reason.

LUKE. Because I'm telling you. Because I'm actually a person and I'm / telling you

ALICE. Well no because what do you want me to say? Because our home is here, my work is here, Henri is here, our life is here / and

LUKE. Not my life

ALICE. Yes our life

LUKE. Not my life

JENNY. Could come and live with me.

ALICE. What?

JENNY. For a bit, he could. You could come and... if you wanted because we've got the, Amy's room, haven't we so.

ALICE. I don't think so.

JENNY. No, you know just to

ALICE. I mean / that's a very kind offer but

JENNY. put it on the table in case.

ALICE. I don't think that's an option for us but that's kind. That's very / kind

JENNY. I'm not on a register you know.

LUKE. Whoa!

JENNY. I am allowed to look after children.

LUKE. *Okay well I'm not a child so.

ALICE. *I just don't think it's ideal, anyway this is the wrong time to, you're tired, I'm tired, you must be, are you hungry?

LUKE. No.

ALICE. Do you want a cheese toastie?

LUKE. No.

ALICE. Do you want an egg in a cup?

LUKE. I want to go back to England.

ALICE. You've said, why?

LUKE. Because my entire life is over.

,

My entire life / is

ALICE. But *why*?

LUKE. Oh my God. Oh my God. Oh my God. Oh / my God.

ALICE. You're not being rational.

LUKE. Can you hear yourself? Can you actually hear yourself?

ALICE. What's happened? Has something / else?

LUKE. No. Yes. No, I dunno.

,

ohhhh, fucking hell

ALICE. Please don't swear at me.

LUKE. That wasn't at you. How was that at you?

ALICE (*going out*). I have to call the police.

LUKE. Why?

ALICE. To tell them you're not bloody dead! To apologise for using their resources! To try and persuade them not to press charges so that you don't end up in prison, actually.

LUKE. As if they would.

ALICE. They would! They would! You assaulted a boy with a weapon! What happened?

A long pause.

He looks at her. Tries to find a way to recount the events of the last scene.

But to do so is unthinkable.

He gives up.

LUKE. They put a razor in my locker.

,

ALICE. Why?

LUKE. Why d'you think?

ALICE. I don't know. I can't, that's horrible. A razor? I'm sorry. I'll tell the headmistress, listen to me, listen, I know you're, but it's going to be okay. I've already spoken to the boy's mother / and

LUKE. Stefan?

ALICE. Stefan, yes, and the school say, his mother says, if you make a formal apology / then

LUKE. I'm not doing that.

ALICE. then they'll let you off / with a suspension so

LUKE. Not in a million years am I doing that

ALICE. You broke his nose! You don't have to do anything, it's all arranged, one meeting and this'll all go away. Okay?

LUKE. He beat me up. He threw bottles at me.

ALICE. Well and I feel sorry for him, because there are people who, that's the only way they know how to deal with the world, but that is not who we are, okay? That is not what I've taught you. You have to rise above them, I'll make you a toastie, you don't have to eat it

KAREN *enters as* LUKE *storms out.*

JENNY. Did you mean that?

ALICE. What? Luke!

JENNY. About me, about me going home.

,

ALICE. You've been so great Jen but. He's back now. And he just needs a calm, a safe space / just to

JENNY. I'm calm. / I'm safe.

ALICE. and you probably want to get back to your own bed / and

KAREN. Could I say something here?

ALICE *and* JENNY. No.

JENNY. Please Alice. Please don't make me

ALICE. Not making you. Not making you, I'm *asking* you. He doesn't like you being here. It gets him / worked up

JENNY. Is it the smoking? Cos I won't, I can just go / outside if

ALICE. it's not the smoking, / it's

JENNY. then what about, no, because we could, we could, we could all go.

ALICE. What?

JENNY. You could come back with me.

ALICE. I don't... I don't think so.

JENNY. England's changed. It's better now. You can get good coffee.

ALICE. It's not really about / the

JENNY. Is it because of your work?

ALICE. Because, no, because of lots of things, I have a son, in school, / who

JENNY. He doesn't want to live here. He hates it, you heard him, what are you doing?

KAREN *has put her arms around* JENNY. JENNY *stiffens*.

KAREN. I'm comforting you.

JENNY. Why?

KAREN. Because it's very hard for me, to watch you argue like this, because you won't win my darling. You're not her intellectual equal.

JENNY. *What?

ALICE. *Mum.

JENNY *wriggles out of her arms*.

KAREN. Of *course* it's because of her work. Of course it is, don't make her justify it. She isn't a brilliant woman.

She's very *clever* but she isn't brilliant. But science is a team sport and she understands her *place*, Jenny. It should be clear to you that what you're asking is impossible. I saw it. What they've built, it's magnificent. Really. But someone like you could never hope to understand *why*. And it's so painful to watch you try, it breaks my heart.

Pause.

ALICE. Yeah. Not sure that's helpful. I have to call the police.

ALICE *goes out.*

A pause.

KAREN *tries to hug* JENNY *again,* JENNY *flinches away from her.*

LUKE *marches in with a sleeping bag.*

JENNY. You can have your room. Your gran and I can sleep out here.

LUKE *rubs his cheek where* ALICE *hit him.*

She thought she was gonna have to watch them drag a lake for you. That's why she gave you a smack. Cos of that. Cos she loves you.

LUKE *stares at her. Dumps the sleeping bag, goes out again.*

KAREN. Goodness me. *Love.* Everyone thinks love is the greatest force in the cosmos and it isn't you know. The greatest force in the cosmos is the Nuclear Strong Force, love's about twelve things down the list after gravity and superglue – actually it's not even a force, not really. It's just something we invented to help us survive chaos and

As she speaks, the scene changes around her, until we find ourselves in…

A TIME OF GREAT CHAOS

> *...very low light.* JENNY *and* KAREN *in sleeping bags.*
> KAREN *sitting upright. In a dream state but she is talking
> to* THE BOSON *who sits in the chair she occupied in the
> previous scene. We can see his outline but he is only a dark
> figure.*

KAREN. and because you know *everyone* always thinks they're
living at a time of great chaos and there was peace once upon
a time if only they could get back to it but chaos came before
us, we came from chaos and that's what we go back to, being
burnt, or worms eating our, until every single atom in our
body is separate from every single other atom and because
that's what death really is, when the gravity that held you
together finally goes for good

THE BOSON *crosses his legs.*

exactly, for example I had three babies, the first one came
out in the lavatory when it was five weeks old while I was
cooking my first Christmas dinner as a married woman,
I hadn't even known so I flushed it, I flushed him or her
away and went on with the bread sauce or whatever, funny
you'd think it would take years to get over something like
that but it didn't really and then after Alice was born for nine
days I went mad. This wasn't unpleasant at first, I had a great
feeling of enlightenment, I gave away nearly four hundred
pounds to various charities and had intense conversations
with a picture of Clint Eastwood about the major issues of
the day and I could read minds, hm yes I could, and Alice
was a mushroom I was tending with milk and flannels. On
the eighth day they discovered the infection and took me
back to hospital, only I thought they were wheeling me to the
crematorium because I was dead and so was Alice and that
was, that's the only time I've ever felt close to

chaos, yes

JENNY *wakes. Sits up, rubs her eyes. Gets up and goes out,
scratching her arse.*

a sort of inescapable terror because effect did not follow
cause and, because all this about infusing the milk for bread

sauce, I don't think it matters and then the antibiotics started to work and in three days / I was alright again

JENNY *returns with a glass of water. Gets back into bed.*

JENNY. Mum, shut up. Mum, you're talking in your sleep, lie down.

THE BOSON *exits. He is not visible to* JENNY.

KAREN. There was a man here.

JENNY. You wish. Lie down.

KAREN *lies down.*

KAREN. I do wish actually. I do wish. I've always preferred the company of men. They put me in a house full of silly bitches, I wish I was dead. She won't live to an old age you know.

JENNY. Who?

KAREN. Jenny. She won't live.

JENNY. Mum it's me. I'm Jenny. Don't –

KAREN. Don't tell me don't, I saw it in her, even as a baby. She was all fat and no gristle. I hope I'm wrong. I hope I go first. It's a hideous thing, to outlive your child.

Pause.

JENNY. I think that's. I think you're wrong.

KAREN. Well, you're a hopeful creature. Hold me.

KAREN *puts her head on* JENNY's *lap.* JENNY *cradles her.*
KAREN *drifts into deep sleep.*
JENNY *sits in the silence. There is nothing else.*
JENNY *sobs silently. Her body convulses violently but she doesn't make any noise.*
Some time. Her phone starts to ring. She grabs it, silences the tone, answers.

JENNY. Hi. Why are you

The person on the other end talks for a long time, she listens.

Okay. Okay. Okay but. What's the Nataraja?

ACT FOUR

NATARAJA

As the scene changes, JENNY *remains and* LUKE *enters. They are in the dark, outside CERN.* THE BOSON *drags on the statue of the Nataraja, depicting Shiva as the cosmic dancer.* THE BOSON *goes.*

LUKE. I need you to take me back to England with you. You need to book me a flight, I don't have a credit card, my passport's in the big drawer, and you can just tell Alice this is just what's happening. Okay? You can just tell her.

JENNY. Yeah, I don't. I'm not sure I can do that.

,

I mean I think it's a discussion we'd have to have with / your

LUKE. No but she doesn't understand. She just does not get the *stupidity* I have to live with, I hope someone walks into the cafeteria one day and shoots them all while they're eating their fucking quiche.

LUKE *breaks down. A deep distress, he sobs and takes deep shuddering breaths.*

JENNY. Yeah well that's. Understandable but I think this is trespassing so, let's go and then we can

She tries to lead him away. But LUKE *refuses to move.*

what happened!

LUKE. I just *told* you.

JENNY. No but what actually happened?

LUKE *gathers his courage. Starts to say something. Stops himself. Starts to say something again. Stops himself. A sound of embarrassment. A deep breath.*

LUKE. You can't tell Alice.

JENNY. I won't tell Alice.

LUKE. No but you can't say that now and then later / on

JENNY. I don't tell Alice anything.

  LUKE *takes a deep breath.*

LUKE. Okay. Okay so I went to this girl's house and she we we like oh my God this is so, gaaaaaah, we

JENNY. you had sex.

LUKE. yeah and because well no not like actually but we like

JENNY. did stuff

LUKE. yeah and she sent this picture of me, of my like... you know

JENNY. oh shit.

LUKE. yeah to everyone, / like

JENNY. fuck

LUKE. everyone exactly like the whole... world and now it's, they can just because I can't do anything to

JENNY. Okay so just calm down

LUKE. No but I can't do anything. I can't do anything.
  ,
  D'you understand what I'm, I / can't

JENNY. Yeah, no, I. I understand.
  ,
  Was it the girl you liked?

LUKE. Yeah.

JENNY. The one you told me about?

LUKE. Yeah.

JENNY. What a bitch. What a fucking, I hope she gets multiple sclerosis.
  ,
  Alright. D'you wanna show me, or?

LUKE. What?

She gestures to his crotch. He stares at her.

Oh my God, what is actually wrong with you?

JENNY. What? You just showed it to half of Geneva, and I've seen it before, you were a very naked / child

LUKE. I'm not getting my cock out for you.

JENNY. Get it out, who said get it out? I don't want to *touch* it

LUKE. this is, / this is literally so

JENNY. I'm not *asking you out*, I'm not *Barbara Windsor*

LUKE. I don't know who that is so

JENNY. I'm just offering to give you a second *opinion* because it's possible actually that this is not the end of the world, it's on your phone, right?

LUKE wrestles with this. Finally, in an agony, he unlocks his phone. Shows her. She looks at the photo. Scientific detachment. Nods. Solemn.

Okay so that's a great cock.

She hands his phone back. He makes a sound of mortification.

No, listen to me: that is a really fantastic cock. Seriously, I've seen thirty-nine in real life and that's way better than basically all of them, you should be really proud. That's a fact, okay? That is a *fact*, if anyone's laughing it's cos they're jealous, fuck 'em.

LUKE. Okay well, you wouldn't tell me anyway so.

JENNY. No I would. I would cos it wouldn't be helpful to you to pretend. Honestly, that is a stellar dick, people *should* see it, Uncle Mike used to show his to black women on the internet and it's like half as big and actually quite repulsive looking. You're lucky. The world is lucky that that cock exists and it's attached to a really good person.

Pause. LUKE is still mortified but now also calmer.

I do get it. I do. But your mum'd never talk to me again if I just took you. And I don't think I could... cope with that right now, / so

LUKE. Please. Please though.

JENNY. No because we'll talk to her, I'll help you talk / to

LUKE. It's too late.

JENNY. Why?

,

Why is it / too

LUKE takes ALICE*'s laptop out of his backpack, shows her.*

LUKE. It's Alice's.

JENNY. So? You took her stuff, you're her kid, that's what happens when you have kids, they take your stuff, we'll just put it back and...

He opens the laptop. Shows her. The screen is frozen and corrupted.

...did you put something on here?

,

LUKE. She doesn't listen to me.

JENNY. What did you put on here?

,

Luke / what did you put on here?

LUKE. I just wanted her to actually, a worm.

JENNY. A worm.

LUKE. yes a worm, a worm, a virus. Okay? I attached it to an email and went in through the CERN network so

JENNY. so, so

LUKE. yeah and I sent it to her whole address book and.

JENNY. fucking hell

LUKE. yeah I know it's really bad

JENNY. is this a joke? Is this like a, because you'll destroy her. You'll completely destroy her.

LUKE. yeah, that was the, that was kind of the

,

I mean that was the whole. Cos then maybe she'd understand.

Pause.

JENNY. Okay let's go. Before / someone

LUKE. I told you, I'm / not

JENNY. no seriously Luke, after that thing at school, they find us here, with that, you'll go to jail. You'll go to, you'll go to *Swiss jail* which I bet, it's probably five times as boring as normal jail. So we / should, let's go.

LUKE. I don't care. I'd rather go to jail for the rest of my life than spend another day at that school.

JENNY. Yeah well you're a teenager so that probably sounds like a really cool thing to say, but / the reality is it'd fuck up your entire life, so I think there's, that is not a, I think we need to think of a different plan.

LUKE. Like what?

JENNY. Yeah, I don't know.

A helpless pause.

LUKE *smashes up the laptop.*

Okay well I think it's a bit late for that but.

JENNY *watches until he is still.*

D'you think she's backed up / cos

GUARD (*off, distant*). Hallo? Qui est là?

JENNY. okay. Shit, no it's, / I'm

LUKE *drops to the floor, scrambles to collect the pieces of laptop.*

LUKE. Fuck.

JENNY. thinking / I'm

LUKE. Shit. Shit.

JENNY. thinking no it's okay. Listen to me: everything's going to be alright. I am not going to let anything happen to you. Okay? Leave that – (*The laptop.*)

LUKE. I don't think / this is

She shoves money at him. A torch beam sweeps across them.

JENNY. No, we're not having a discussion. You're a child, I'm a grown up, I'm telling you, take that, get a taxi, go home. Get into bed. You don't tell Alice. This is just between us.

GUARD (*off*). Vous êtes sur une propriété privée!

LUKE. what are you going to

JENNY. Doesn't matter, just go.

LUKE. yeah but

JENNY. I love you

LUKE. it's

JENNY. very much.
   I loved it when you played with her on the blue rug.
   The thing with the sock. The pair of you.

LUKE. Jenny.

JENNY. I know

LUKE. No but / I

JENNY. I know.
   I know.
   I know.
   Okay.
   Fuck off then.

GUARD. Arrêtez! Arrêtez!

LUKE *runs. A searchlight flashes across* JENNY.

She looks into it. Puts up her hands. A SECURITY GUARD *enters.*

JENNY. Bon soir. Um. Parlez-vous anglais?

Behind her, Shiva starts to dance.

Sudden black. In the dark, a terrifying wall of sound. A vast cloud of helium tearing through the largest machine in the world, concrete torn up, magnets ripped from anchors, metal tearing, alarms blaring as an emergency shutdown is triggered.

QUENCH

Interview room, police station. JENNY at a table. ALICE sits across from her, holding her bag on her lap, coat on. A POLICEWOMAN sits, apart, engrossed in her phone. ALICE stares at JENNY for some time, then:

ALICE. What happened?

JENNY....

ALICE. Okay well I need you to explain it to me. Because it doesn't make any sense I can't

understand it and I need to

understand it so so so you need to explain it to me because right now I am...

how did you even do it?

JENNY. What d'you mean?

ALICE. I mean, given your PIN number is 1234, how did you manage / to

JENNY. I got it off Luke. It's not his fault. He didn't know. Sorry.

Pause.

ALICE. Is that it?

Pause. ALICE stands.

Fine. I have to (jesus) I have to go to work so.

JENNY. Now?

ALICE. Yes now, there's been a quench. The whole thing's shut down. It's like a disaster movie, magnets ripped from / the

JENNY. Oh my God. And. But. Did I do that?

ALICE stares at her.

ALICE. There is not a single piece of machinery in that building simple enough for you to destroy it. Even the hand-dryers would defeat you.

JENNY. It wasn't my fault?

ALICE. We *invented the internet* Jenny. I think our IT system can withstand a middle-aged woman having a tantrum.

JENNY. So… but what caused it then?

ALICE. We don't know. We think maybe an electrical fault. There seem to be some… faulty connections.

JENNY. It's only been running a week, how is that even?

ALICE. A hundred million active parts. Something was bound to go wrong.

The POLICEWOMAN *laughs at something on her phone.* ALICE *and* JENNY *look at her. She looks up briefly, unapologetic, then back down again.*

What have they told you?

JENNY. No one's told me anything. They brought me a croissant.

She shows her. Bangs it on the table to show how hard and stale it is.

ALICE. They're deciding whether to press charges.

JENNY. Right. D'you think they will / or

ALICE. I don't know. I explained it all.

JENNY. What did you explain?

ALICE. What did I *explain*?

JENNY. No, like. How you explain it?

ALICE. I explained that you're in a state of emotional distress.

I explained that you're not very clever.

I explained that you're a mad bitch who believes everything she reads on the internet, and that the combination of these things caused you to behave like a fucking peasant.

The POLICEWOMAN*'s phone starts to ring. Jaunty. She goes out.*

Pause. JENNY *tries to take a bite of croissant. It's too hard. She puts it down.*

JENNY. I wish you'd told me.

ALICE. I am, I'm telling you right now, you're a fucking peasant.

JENNY. No, I mean. You never told me.

,

ALICE. What?

JENNY. What?

ALICE. I never told you what?

JENNY. That I should, you know, I should give her the, I should give her it.

,

ALICE. It? The vaccination? Are / you

JENNY. You never said, and I just wish. Cos I'd've listened to you.

ALICE. Because it was obvious. / It was, this is not, we are not having this

JENNY. Yeah no, I wasn't trying to, it was a compliment I was saying, / you're the only person I would have

ALICE. No you're not. You're pretending it's a compliment, when actually you're saying it's my fault, / how is it my

JENNY. No, just, Mum told me and Mike told me but you were just, oh it's your decision Jen, think for yourself / and I think maybe

ALICE. Don't *put* this on me. Don't you dare put this on me because there's Progress and there's Horror, and you chose Horror Jen, you *chose* it

JENNY. It's not that simple.

ALICE. Yes it is. It really is.

JENNY. Yeah well try telling that to Mark Falshaw.

ALICE. Who?

JENNY. Mark Falshaw! You know! We used to play football /
with him.

ALICE. Are you talking about Thalidomide?

JENNY. A person can ask questions, that's all I'm saying, a /
person can

ALICE. It's a *vaccination*, of course you give your child a /
vaccination

JENNY. Yeah but you never *told* me that, that's / all I'm

ALICE. Because I assumed you had! Because I assumed no one could be that stupid, it's not like an optional fucking thing, it's what you do, / it's like feeding them and washing them

JENNY. Okay but can I just say something? Can I just say something?

ALICE. it's the twenty-first century, it's what you *do*, you *child*

JENNY. Hang on

ALICE. You *cripple*

JENNY. Hey. / HEY.

ALICE. You know Jen, you're exactly the person they print 'caution: hot liquids' on coffee cups for. It's amazing to me how you ever

ALICE *cuts herself dead.*

,

JENNY. What?

ALICE. No, I just meant maybe you, maybe you just.

,

JENNY. What?

ALICE. Maybe it's… in the long run. Maybe you weren't… cut out for it.

,

JENNY. For being. For being a

,

I am cut out. I am so cut out. What do I do all day with Mum? You think that's some sort of pleasure for me, I'm some sort of, lady's companion, do I look like Joan fucking Fontaine? I *mother* her, I am her *mother* I take her to the toilet and I wash her clothes and iron the clothes and put her back in them, and I, I am a good mother, I am a good mother to her.

ALICE. Fine all I'm saying is / maybe it's a responsibility you weren't – sorry I'm talking. I am actually still talking Jenny

JENNY. I'm not cut *out*? Who *says* that, I need some qualification, some letters after my name, I gave *birth* to her, they pulled her *out* of me, that's my *qualification*, not cut out for, you can talk, Luke hates your guts love. He *ran away*, doesn't say two words to you, 'oh my son doesn't do drugs, he doesn't drink', he stole my fucking Crème de Menthe, didn't he, good luck to him I say, have a drink son, I would if I / was your

ALICE. When?

JENNY. What?

ALICE. When did he steal it? Did he come back from school?

JENNY. I don't know.

ALICE. So when did you see him steal it?

JENNY. It was gone, I just assumed… maybe he didn't. I don't know.

ALICE *is staring at her. A realisation.*

ALICE. I asked you. How many times did I ask you if you'd seen him?

JENNY. Maybe Henri… maybe I drank it.

ALICE. Stop it. Why did he run away? What did you say to my son?

JENNY. I never. I didn't mean it. Allie…

ALICE. Why did you lie? Why did you lie?

Pause.

JENNY. I thought you'd shout at me.

ALICE *stares at the table for a really long time. Eventually:*

*Okay, look:

ALICE. *There's this security guard at work. The head of security, he used to be in the army and he – Nico, his name is Nico, Nico gives us talks on what to do if a gunman enters the facility which, I find it really hard to get through them without laughing because he takes it so seriously.

He says first of all: *you* have the advantage. You know the geography of the building. Use this knowledge to evade the gunman and barricade yourself in your office. Second, he says:

The group is as slow as its slowest member.

But you cannot allow the slowest member to put your life at risk.

Your instinct will be to help them, because they're weaker or younger or older or more frightened than you.

Don't.

Leave them behind.

If they're lucky they'll find a place of concealment.

For example under a desk, or a low cupboard.

And then he makes us all practise breathing completely silently for ten minutes and then we all go back to work.

,

JENNY. Okay so can I / just

ALICE. So this happens about once a year, this speech, and every time I hear it, when he says 'the group is as slow as its slowest member', it makes me think of you. Because I spend

all day with some of the cleverest people in the world then
I get home and my inbox is full of messages from a retard.

JENNY. 'Scuse me, no, nine days your machine has been
running and the whole thing shuts down cos you fuck the
wiring up, and I'm the retard am I?

ALICE. Yes.

JENNY. I'm the retard?

ALICE. Yes.

JENNY. I'm the retard?

ALICE. Yes.

JENNY. How's that work then?

ALICE. Because the only thing that makes us worth anything is
that we try to be less stupid and you don't fucking bother.

JENNY. I am not stupid. I am not stupid.

ALICE. No, to be honest Jen it's not that you're stupid really
but more that you're completely devoted to being stupid.
You worship it. I think you might actually be quite proud of
it. And I don't, I'm finding that more and more frightening,
actually. So I think that might be it.

JENNY. What?

ALICE. I think... I might be done. Yeah.

,

JENNY. But I'm.

ALICE. I know. I'm sorry.

    ALICE *gets up to leave*.

JENNY. Alice please. Sit down, you have to, you have to

ALICE. I have to? Why do I have to? What is the reason I have
to? Blood?

Because actually I think if the world's going to get better
and not worse then Nico might have a point. He's mad, he
has PTSD, he lives in his car, in a quarry, but I think he
might be right, maybe that's all we can do with you. Just

leave you behind. Go on ahead. Maybe you'll find a place
of concealment.

The POLICEWOMAN *returns.*

POLICEWOMAN. Time is over, please.

ALICE. Thank you. Merci.

JENNY. What so you're just going? I'm here and you're / just

ALICE. Yes well that's it isn't it? You're here. We have to share
a world with you, and because you're weak, you think that
means you're powerless but actually, actually, and this is
what really frightens me

POLICEWOMAN. Scusez-moi, allez-y…

ALICE. actually you're a very powerful woman Jenny yes,
thank you, I'm coming.

    ALICE *turns,* JENNY *reaches for her.*

JENNY. I want to speak to Luke. I need / to

    ALICE *turns like a tiger. Incandescent.*

ALICE. NO! No. You don't come anywhere near him. I mean it.
I really mean that, I'll never speak to you again, I'm not
joking. Okay? (*To the* POLICEWOMAN.) I'd like you to
keep this woman away from me, please, thank you.

POLICEWOMAN. Qu'est-ce qui s'est passé?

ALICE. What?

POLICEWOMAN. Does she threaten you?

ALICE. (oh, yes) she does threaten me, she threatens all of us.
She's the fucking apocalypse.

    (*To the* POLICEWOMAN, *gathered.*) Sorry. Sorry about that.

    ALICE *goes. The* POLICEWOMAN *looks at* JENNY.

JENNY. She's just upset. She's not. She doesn't.

    She holds up the croissant.

    This is completely inedible.

    Sudden black.

A HIGGS JET, DECAYING

LUKE *at home as* ALICE *enters. He looks up, but she doesn't look at him. She has been crying but is not crying now. She finds* JENNY*'s handbag, empties it on the floor. She finds what she is looking for, a packet of fags. She lights one. Smokes.*

LUKE *stares at her. He has never seen her smoke before. A small, involuntary cough.*

ALICE *turns her eyes to him. Stares. Looks away. Smokes. Pause.*

LUKE *puts his headphones on* ALICE. *Plays a track from his laptop.* ALICE *listens to the music he has made with the sounds of particles colliding. We hear it too. She is captivated. When she looks at him, she sees* THE BOSON.

LUKE. What?

ALICE. Nothing.

ALICE *puts out her cigarette and listens. The track finishes. Silence. Then:*

Play it again.

Sudden black.

ALICE *exits.* LUKE *remains.* THE BOSON *nearly exits but turns back.*

THE LAST EXPERIMENT

THE BOSON. By the way, there is one other way for the world to end. And that is Luke Mabey.

Decades after the Higgs boson has been discovered, after the Nobel Prizes have been handed out, Luke is working at a different particle collider in Long Island. He has a happy but complicated marriage, two beautiful daughters and on a [warm evening] in [July], he is in a cinema with his girls, watching *Captain Underpants 4*.

Lately he's been struggling with an equation. It isn't E equals MC squared, we're not talking Special Relativity. But it's important to him and he's been banging his head on it. But it's dark in here. The air is cool. The conditions are perfect for his mind to go completely blank.

LUKE *stares ahead. His brain detached from his body. Thinking.*

And by the time the lights come up, he's solved it. It's a small step forward. His colleagues are pleased. There are beers after work. But Luke will win no prizes, no buildings are named after him and he dies eighteen years later of bowel cancer.

But the modest discovery that takes place in Luke's brain that night has got legs. It blossoms. It's the scientific equivalent of eggs. Unspectacular in itself, but crucial to a surprisingly large number of recipes. Other scientists use Luke's equation, build on it, it grows and evolves and mutates and unfolds until centuries later

As he speaks, a basement laboratory in a disused theatre in the future appears. A number of SCIENTISTS. THE BOSON *can see them but they cannot see him.*

in a flooded city, in a makeshift laboratory in a disused theatre, in a ruined world, a team of scientists work late into the night, attempting to harness enough energy to punch through into another dimension, where they hope to birth a new universe exactly like this one. It is the most important attempt at IVF in human history. And time is running out.

But on the thirty-fourth attempt, after many years of heartbreak and hope and passive-aggressive rows and silent breakfasts, they are successful.

They open a viewing window. On the other side of it, a portal has opened up.

Celebration. They embrace and gather to watch, tense.

And then they wait, and watch, and through this portal, they observe the conception of the second Big Bang.

There is nothing. Nothing explodes.

Another small celebration. The scientists keep watching, as 13.75 billion years of the universe's evolution appears to happen in fifty-three seconds.

It plays out exactly like the first time round

as unimaginable amounts of energy are released

as something comes of nothing

all matter is plasma, a pea-souper that lasts three hundred thousand years

the Higgs field forms, gives particles mass

the universe becomes transparent

elements are born

stars

a thin disc of galaxy that looks strangely familiar

followed by a solar system

and finally in front of them there is an embryo

A planet, the size of an apple

not because it is small, but because it is far away

not because it is small, but because it is far away

now it comes closer, and closer

it grows and grows

its proud, anxious parents watch as asteroids rain down on it

oceans boil

life appears and multiplies

trees, lichen, crabs, ferns, sea urchins, dinosaurs, mosquitoes, hagfish, ratfish, parrots, loons and short-faced bears

and but because this process is taking place in a dimension with a completely different sense of time from ours, to the scientists watching, this process appears to happen in *under a minute.*

Some of the SCIENTISTS *are crying. Others watch with their hands over their mouths.*

Some of them want to hold each other. Some of them want to be alone.

Fourteen billion years pass in fifty-three seconds

as chaos congeals into something that looks

a

lot

like

home.

And these scientists – and by the way as people, they are really as different as it's possible to be, it's unthinkable for them to be united in anything and yet and yet as they stand there, turning off the lights of the old world, preparing to step through this portal into a new one, they are all thinking exactly the same thing, they are looking at this lush this fecund this generous blue-green carbon copy they have created, the child that will allow them to go on living, and they have the impossible delusional indulgent but nonetheless necessary thought that any creator has, they think

this time

this time

this time

we're going to get it right.

The SCIENTISTS *grab suitcases, plants and equipment and step through the portal.*

THE BOSON *looks around at the old, abandoned world. Sudden black.*

SFB

November 2008. England. Behind a pub. ALICE *perches on a stack of beer crates, waiting.* JENNY *enters with two half pints of orange juice. Gives one to* ALICE.

JENNY. Sorry about that. Manager's a bell-end. She's about twelve. Can't even pull a pint of Guinness properly.

JENNY sits on a stack of crates. ALICE *rummages in a plastic duty-free bag.*

ALICE. Um, I brought you…

She pulls out a carton of cigarettes.

JENNY. Oh, no, thanks, but. Given up.

Pause.

Go on, give us one then. No, don't. Fucking hell it's boring isn't it? People talking about their addictions, it is, it's fucking boring, it's as bad as dreams. It's, all it is, is it's something to do with your hands, isn't it? That's, it just makes me really aware of my hands which.

Pause. JENNY *takes* ALICE*'s hand. Neither of them acknowledges this.*

Thanks for coming.

ALICE. No, that's. You said you had something to tell me

JENNY. Oh. / Okay but

ALICE. because I'm still, I'm still so angry / but

JENNY lets go of her hand.

JENNY. I know

ALICE. I know you know, but I thought, I felt if you were ready, to explain, what happened that night then we might be able to, because it still doesn't make sense to me, it doesn't make sense that you could hate me so / much

JENNY. I don't

ALICE. no but that you could have such, such *spite* towards me and, and my work, to want to, to destroy me like that and because I don't hate you. I don't hate you at all. I don't understand you but I don't hate you, and then I got your email and it was full of light and it was full of love and I was so happy. I was so happy, sorry, and but what I wanted to say is that I know how hard this must be for you and I respect you for that, no, I do, and whatever you have to say, however, you know, I am ready to hear it.

JENNY. Right. Yeah. It's.

She takes a deep breath.

Sorry, just I'm not sure / I really

ALICE. It's okay. Take your time. Take as much time as you.

Pause. ALICE *touches her own cheek, suppressing a wave of pain.*

JENNY. How's Luke?

ALICE. He's. Actually he's good, / he's

JENNY. Good, that's good.

ALICE. Yeah, he's moved schools, he's much better. He wanted to come today actually which I / thought was

JENNY. Did he?

ALICE. Yes, but I thought, I didn't think you'd want him to see you like this.

JENNY. 'Like this'? This is how I am, I don't mind. Should bring him, next time. How's the, what about the Collider?

ALICE. We're still repairing it. Hoping to be online again within the year, what?

JENNY is smiling.

JENNY. No just, it frightens me actually. Your brain. Mike says in twenty years every job I'm qualified to do will be done by an algorithm invented by someone like you. Do you think that's true?

ALICE. Maybe. Probably. I don't know.

JENNY. Fucking hell. D'you know what I mean though? Fucking hell.

Pause.

ALICE. So?

JENNY sighs.

Sorry, rushing / you, it's fine

JENNY. Why do you even need to know?

ALICE. Because I need to.

JENNY. Yeah, well you can't know everything, can you?

ALICE. What?

JENNY. You just can't. Even those bitches on Mumsnet don't know everything, they still talk about me you know. They've got an acronym and everything. SFB, they call me.

ALICE. I don't

JENNY. Shit For Brains.

ALICE. That's not / very

JENNY. No it's not is it? But there you go, expect I make them feel better about themselves, when they're having an MC, or an EP, or they're TTC or whatever. That's all it is really.

'

ALICE. What's TTC?

JENNY. Trying To Conceive. Do you want to get some lunch?

Pause. ALICE stands.

Cos there's a Pret, round / the

ALICE. I'm an idiot, aren't I?

JENNY. Don't do / that

ALICE. No, I am, I'm a moron, one email you probably wrote
while you were pissed and I get on a plane, I cancelled
a dentist appointment for this, I have an abscess, I'm on /
codeine

JENNY. Alice.

ALICE. and you can't even, what?

JENNY. Do you still pray for me?

ALICE. To be honest Jenny, no I don't. Not any more.

JENNY nods. ALICE pulls her coat on.

JENNY. I'm pregnant.

A very long pause.

ALICE. No.

JENNY. Yeah. Yes. That's what I wanted to, I'm pregnant.

A long pause.

ALICE. How many, how many months?

JENNY. Um, four. Four and a week.

ALICE. So you were… when Amy died… you were already?

JENNY. Uh-huh.

ALICE. With Mike?

JENNY. Don't rub it in.

ALICE. No but is he

JENNY. He's taking some time. He's having a think

ALICE. and so, sorry, this is it, is it, this is what was so /
important I had to

JENNY. felt weird. Not telling you

ALICE. oh well if it felt *weird* then. Okay. Okay well
presumably you're going to, I mean I think you have to

JENNY. What?

ALICE. don't you think?

JENNY. What?

ALICE. well don't make me say it

JENNY. No but what are you saying?

ALICE. You know what I'm saying.

JENNY. Oh.

ALICE. Yes.

JENNY. Oh!

ALICE. Because

JENNY (*Dalek*). Exterminate.

ALICE. No don't, it's not. Don't, seriously, don't, because you took all those pills. You were permanently pissed, you were *wasted* for about two months, charcoal and and and and smoking / like a

JENNY. I know, it's mental, it should be just a ball of fingers. Doctor says it's alright though.

,

ALICE. You've had the ultrasound?

JENNY. Had one. Got to go back for another one. Find out the

ALICE. gender.

JENNY. yeah.

Pause.

ALICE. And it's… okay / is it?

JENNY. Yeah. Far as they can

ALICE. But it can't be… it can't be… it can't / be

JENNY. No, but it is. It is. It's perfect.

Pause.

ALICE. I just have to say

JENNY. Can we not

ALICE. I really think / this is

JENNY. Just I feel like we've covered this, and I don't want you to say something you can't take back so.

ALICE. I think it's unhinged

JENNY. There it is.

JENNY sits.

ALICE. and psychotic, you're on your own.

JENNY. Well…

ALICE. No, I'm telling you, you are on your own.

ALICE sits. A plane goes overhead. JENNY looks up at it.
Her eyes follow a bird as it flies into her vision and lands.
She salutes three times.

JENNY. Good morning mr magpie good morning mr magpie good morning mr magpie.

ALICE joins in the final salute.
ALICE sits beside JENNY.
JENNY puts ALICE's hands on her stomach. Holds them there.
Above us and around us the whoomph of ultrasound waves as loud as a train coming into a station
deafening, terrifying
the sound of JENNY breathing
a hum of mosquitoes
and our heartbeat, growing louder
as the experiment begins.

End.

MANHATTAN THEATRE CLUB

Manhattan Theatre Club

Under the dynamic leadership of Artistic Director Lynne Meadow and Executive Producer Barry Grove, Manhattan Theatre Club has grown in four-and-a-half decades from a prolific Off-Off-Broadway showcase into one of the United States's most acclaimed theatre organisations.

MTC's many laurels include 20 Tony Awards, 6 Pulitzer Prizes, 48 Obies and 33 Drama Desk Awards, as well as numerous Drama Critics Circle, Outer Critics Circle and Theatre World Awards. MTC has won the Lucille Lortel Award for Outstanding Achievement, a Drama Desk for Outstanding Excellence, and a Theatre World for Outstanding Achievement.

Founded in 1970, MTC is committed to the creation of new plays and musicals through an intensive Artistic Development Program that offers commissions, script evaluation, dramaturgical support, readings and workshops. Using the work on its stages, MTC's Education Program promotes active participation in the arts through in-class instruction, student and family matinees, teacher training, internships and internet-based distance learning. In constantly seeking new ways to innovate, MTC keeps theatre alive and relevant.

'A great published script makes you understand what the play is, at its heart' *Slate Magazine*

Enjoyed this book? Choose from hundreds more classic and contemporary plays from Nick Hern Books, the UK's leading independent theatre publisher.

Our full range is available to browse online now, including:

Award-winning plays from leading contemporary dramatists, including *King Charles III* by Mike Bartlett, *Anne Boleyn* by Howard Brenton, *Jerusalem* by Jez Butterworth, *A Breakfast of Eels* by Robert Holman, *Chimerica* by Lucy Kirkwood, *The Night Alive* by Conor McPherson, *The James Plays* by Rona Munro, *Nell Gwynn* by Jessica Swale, and many more...

Ground-breaking drama from the most exciting up-and-coming playwrights, including Vivienne Franzmann, James Fritz, Ella Hickson, Anna Jordan, Jack Thorne, Phoebe Waller-Bridge, Tom Wells, and many more...

Twentieth-century classics, including *Cloud Nine* by Caryl Churchill, *Death and the Maiden* by Ariel Dorfman, *Pentecost* by David Edgar, *Angels in America* by Tony Kushner, *Long Day's Journey into Night* by Eugene O'Neill, *The Deep Blue Sea* by Terence Rattigan, *Machinal* by Sophie Treadwell, and many more...

Timeless masterpieces from playwrights throughout the ages, including Anton Chekhov, Euripides, Henrik Ibsen, Federico García Lorca, Christopher Marlowe, Molière, William Shakespeare, Richard Brinsley Sheridan, Oscar Wilde, and many more...

Every playscript is a world waiting to be explored. Find yours at **www.nickhernbooks.co.uk** – you'll receive a 20% discount, plus free UK postage & packaging for orders over £30.

'Publishing plays gives permanent form to an evanescent art, and allows many more people to have some kind of experience of a play than could ever see it in the theatre' *Nick Hern, publisher*

www.nickhernbooks.co.uk

www.nickhernbooks.co.uk

 facebook.com/nickhernbooks

 twitter.com/nickhernbooks